This Thing of Ours

How Faith Saved My Mafia Marriage

Cammy Franzese

THOMAS NELSON
Since 1798

NASHVILLE DALLAS MEXICO CITY RIO DE JANEIRO

Published in Nashville, Tennessee, by Thomas Nelson. Thomas Nelson is a registered trademark of Thomas Nelson, Inc.

Published in association with the literary agency of Esther Fedorkevich, Fedd and Company Inc., 9759 Concord Pass, Brentwood TN 37027.

Thomas Nelson, Inc., titles may be purchased in bulk for educational, business, fund-raising, or sales promotional use. For information, please e-mail SpecialMarkets@ThomasNelson.com.

All scriptures are taken from the *Holy Bible*, New Living Translation. © 1996. Used by permission of Tyndale House Publishers, Inc., Wheaton, Illinois 60189. All rights reserved.

Library of Congress Cataloging-in-Publication Data

Franzese, Cammy, 1963-
    This thing of ours : how faith saved my Mafia marriage / Cammy Franzese.
      p. cm.
  ISBN 978-1-59555-365-2 (pbk.)
  1. Franzese, Cammy, 1963- 2. Women and the mafia--United States--Case studies. 3. Mafia--United States--Case studies. 4. Wives--United States--Biography. 5. Christian women--United States--Biography. I. Title.
  HV6446.F717 2012
  364.1092--dc23

                      2011033961

Printed in the United States of America

12 13 14 15 16 QGF 6 5 4 3 2 1

Dedication

To my brothers, Dean, Joaquin, Cuauhtemoc, and Che. Half of the "skeleton crew." I will always love you guys and thank God for how He has blessed you all to be serving Him in your ministry. I know Mom continues to smile on you all.

To my sisters, Sabrina and Raquel. We will never replace the hole in our hearts left when Mom went to heaven, but I thank God that we have each other. I love you both so much.

To my dad. I believe Mom has seen her prayers answered with you. You are a terrific grandfather, and I know how much you love all your children. I thank you for helping to make me the woman I am today. I love you, Dad.

To my precious mother. Not a day goes by when I don't think about you and hold back a tear. I miss you so much. Both in this life and in your eternal life, you have been my guardian angel. You have prayed your entire family and my husband into God's grace and service. I know I will see your beautiful face again, Mom. Thank you for being everything to me. I love you more than words can say.

To my Nana and Tata, thank you for all the amazing summers we spent together. They were all very special to me. I love you both so very much.

To my beautiful daughters, Miquelle, Amanda, and Julia. You are all my precious angels. The three of you have been my rock through good times and bad. I would not have made it through all the tough times without you. I am so very proud of you for the young women you have become. I pray that God always keeps us close. I love you all so very much.

To my son, Michael Jr. You were such a joy to me in your childhood, Mike. You gave me so many reasons to smile. I know you have had some struggles, but I also know God will see you through them. I pray for you every day, and I will always be there for you. I love you with all my heart. I am proud to be your mother.

To my husband, Michael. I thank you for loving me as you do. For always putting me first in your life. For staying strong through all of your struggles. For the man you are and for the servant of God you have become. Without you in my life, there would be no story. I love you, forever and ever and always, until death do us part.

Contents

1. Locked Up   1
2. Knights of the City   8
3. Who Is Michael Franzese?   28
4. Together   41
5. Taking the Next Step   45
6. When Everything Started to Change   65
7. Finding Out the Truth   87
8. A New Kind of Life   109
9. Not Again   133
10. Coming Home   153
11. Choices and God's Goodness   174
    Epilogue   194
    Acknowledgments   199

1

Locked Up

I shuffled down the gray corridor, my wrists tightly bound by steel handcuffs that dug into my skin. Silent tears streamed down my face, turning it into a makeup-smeared wetland, and my shoulders were shaking. But I knew I couldn't let my crying be audible. I had to fake some semblance of strength, so I looked straight ahead, making eye contact with no one. The individual jail cells that lined the hallway on each side were brimming with women in the same indistinguishable beige (and very itchy) uniform I was wearing. They didn't hesitate to stare me down and obnoxiously greet me. The mesh of high-pitched voices, giggles, and whistles rang loudly in my ears.

"Hey you, what are you doing here?"

"Lookit that beauty!"

"What are you? A drug dealer? You from Colombia?"

"Nah, she's the wife of a drug dealer."

The women continued their catcalls and sarcastic comments as I was shoved into a private cell. A million thoughts ran through my mind. *What's going on? Does this have anything to do with Michael? And what about the kids? What is going to happen to them? What on earth am I doing here? What am I doing here?*—now, that was the million-dollar question.

Only a few hours earlier I was getting my three children, Miquelle, Amanda, and Michael Jr., up and ready for the day. It was the beginning of 1992, and my husband, notorious mobster Michael Franzese, was in prison for the second time. A former *caporegime* (high-ranking member) in the Colombo crime family, Michael had served four years in jail beginning in 1985, the same year we got married. He had copped a plea to racketeering and conspiracy and was given a ten-year prison sentence. When he got out in 1989, after serving only a partial sentence, he landed himself back in jail thirteen months later on a parole violation. He would stay there another four years. That morning, as I shook my kids out of their nighttime haze, telling them for the umpteenth time to wake up, my husband was sitting in solitary confinement in a prison across town. It was true solitary confinement, mainly for his safety.

A knock interrupted the early-morning frenzy. The kids were still in their rooms, making feeble attempts to get up. When I opened the front door, I was disgusted to find Detective Prieto standing there. I knew him well because of my husband. This guy had been on Michael's tail from the very beginning. Matter of fact, he was the one who had arrested Michael the first time around. He was a very mean and vindictive man who didn't hide the fact that he had it in for our family.

"Camille Franzese, we have a warrant for your arrest," he said without the slightest bit of emotion.

What?

My mouth dropped to the floor, and I started choking up. I heard little Michael call out from his bedroom, "Mommy, who is it? Who's at the door?" My hands shook as I told the detective, "Give me a minute. Let me get the kids taken care of." I left him standing impatiently at the front of my house as I panicked. I had no idea what was going on.

My saving grace was our housekeeper. Ofelia never spent the night at our house, but for some reason, she had stayed with us the night before. I believe it was divine intervention—God's way of preparing me and my family for what was to come. There's been a lot of that in our lives. It's been impossible not to see the hand of Providence sweeping in every which way throughout my journey as Michael's wife and my children's mother.

I had to act fast. I ran up the stairs and found Ofelia opening the curtains in one of the kids' rooms, inviting in the warm sunlight. I asked her to get the kids dressed, drive them to school, and call my mother; Mom would handle everything else. I couldn't say much more and told her I had to leave, that it was an emergency. Ofelia didn't speak English very well, but she could read the panic in my eyes. She nodded and set off to the tasks at hand.

It broke my heart that I couldn't say good-bye to my kids. If they saw me leave with the police, they would no doubt ask a million questions and worry their little hearts out. The last thing I wanted to do was give them one more thing to be upset about.

I ran back down the stairs, grabbed a jacket and my boots, and left the house with the officers, who escorted me to a waiting police car. Sitting in the backseat, I finally broke down and started to cry. Detective Prieto ignored me and started talking loudly to no one in particular, though it was obvious he knew I couldn't help but hear him.

He droned on and on about my husband. "You know, Michael is never going to get out of prison. We've got some information on him. He'll be locked up for good this time." Finally he turned to me, poked his head through the opening in the plastic shield that separates criminal from law enforcer, and said, "You know, you can talk to me, Camille. You can tell me anything you'd like to share." I remember thinking, *Is he that dumb to think I'm going to start rambling on about my husband?* Besides, I didn't have anything to say.

It was a nightmare. I still didn't know why I was arrested. I vaguely recall Detective Prieto mentioning something about a deed with a faulty notary seal and signature. It didn't make any sense. I figured, however, that the legal drama had something to do with Michael. It always did.

In a blur of tears, I was handcuffed and taken into custody at the Sybil Brand Institute, a woman's jail in Los Angeles County. Here's a twist of irony: I happened to be good friends with Sybil Brand. She attended the church Michael and I first attended together. Sybil had converted from Judaism to Christianity and was a well-known philanthropist in town. She had raised a lot of money to build the women's jail because prior to that time, men and women were housed in the same facility. You can imagine the problems that can erupt in a coed prison.

I was placed in a holding cell with an old, skinny woman who constantly talked to herself. My crying interrupted her gibberish. She turned toward me, flashed a grin that displayed just two teeth, and said, "Sweetie, don't cry. Let's talk. So what are you here for, anyway? Drugs?" I burst into another round of tears, still clasping the bologna sandwich one of the officers had given me.

She tried to soothe me again, but my plight was no match for my sandwich. "Hey, you gonna eat that? I'm starvin'!" Between heaving sobs, I handed her the plastic bag. She snatched it and chomped her two teeth with ecstasy right into the bologna. As she chewed, she continued to mumble at me not to worry. *Easy for her to say.*

An hour or so later, I was reassigned to another cell, a private one. It was freezing, and I didn't have any socks on; I had run out of the house in bare feet, holding my boots. I spent the first few minutes in jail shivering and sobbing.

The girl next to my six-by-eight cell had caught a glimpse of my face when I was thrown in. "Hi, honey," she said. "You look familiar. I think I've seen you someplace before." Her voice was sweet and surprisingly articulate.

I hesitated to respond, but it was nice to hear what sounded like a genuinely friendly person. I was grateful for the conversation. "No, I don't think so."

She wouldn't drop the topic. "No, wait. I have. Weren't you featured in *Vanity Fair* or *Life* magazine or something with your husband? Yeah, I remember now. You're the one married to the mafioso, right?"

Bingo. She did know who I was. What a small world. The young woman's name was Nicole. She lived in La Jolla and was the daughter of a prominent, wealthy family. College educated and cultured, she began associating with the wrong kind of people, then messing with drugs. To fuel her habit, she started stealing from her parents and family friends and writing bad checks. But for the entire length of my stay in jail, Nicole was my guardian angel, calming me down and talking me through the ordeal. She somehow even managed to get me a pair of socks and a Reese's Peanut Butter Cup that day.

Nicole told me that the area where our cells were located was a high-profile place. "Believe me: it's much better to be back here than with the others," she reassured me. When she gave me the rundown of the other women who had been sentenced to Sybil, I couldn't believe my ears. The woman in the cell next to mine was there for murdering her husband. Another had killed her children by gassing them with oven fumes. Still another had strangled her boyfriend for drugs. The list went on.

I'm thankful for Nicole. I was an emotional wreck sitting in a jail cell, wondering what I was doing there, when I was going to get out, and worrying about my children. This sweet woman made my stay bearable, offering kind words and telling me about herself. I also felt compassion for her. Criminal or not, she seemed like a lost little girl who'd once had big dreams for herself that crumbled to bits because of a drug addiction. I was so touched by her story that, after I got out, I wrote her a few letters to encourage her.

After twenty-four hours I was released on bail. My mom had taken care of the kids, who were now waiting for me at home. When they asked, "Where's Mom?" she told them I had taken a mini-trip to see Nana in San Diego.

Seeing my babies again brought me such comfort and peace. Hugging them was like embracing a piece of heaven. They were happy to have me home and (thankfully) didn't ask too many questions. I, however, was overwhelmed. It still wasn't clear why charges had been pressed against me, though our lawyer was doing some footwork to find out the details.

Something happened after I was arrested and spent a day in jail—I changed. I was depressed at first and then very angry. I didn't talk to Michael until a day or two after. He was beside himself and kept repeating, "Honey, I'm sorry" over the prison telephone. I was peeved and took my frustration out on him. "I don't know what's going on, but this is unacceptable. This is not just about me, Michael! We have three kids! Do you understand how all this is affecting them?"

The experience changed me in many ways. For years I had kept myself in the dark about Michael's background and his dealings with organized crime. I maintained a level of naive that, in my mind, I needed in order to be a good wife and mother. But now my eyes were slowly becoming accustomed to a different life: A life of doubt and questions. A life of paranoia and worry, of not knowing if I would be whisked away again out of my own home.

Since we'd married, I'd dealt with multiple ongoing federal investigations, FBI agents pounding on our door at odd hours of the day, Michael taking frequent trips to New York for God-knows-what, and, of course, almost eight years of him being behind bars and me visiting several times a week. Whether he was locked up in

New York, Arizona, Colorado, or Chicago—you name the place—I made the trek to see him.

Don't get me wrong. I'm not complaining. I chose to marry Michael even though he had a colorful background (the full extent of which I still don't know). But as a result of my jail experience, the bubble of confidence I once had in him and in our relationship burst. See, I was used to certain things. I was used to Michael fixing things that went wrong. I was used to his reassurances that everything would be okay (because nine times out of ten, it *would*). Michael, in his inimitable way, was always able to work out any problem that came our way.

My being thrown in jail without any known cause, however, was something he couldn't fix. He couldn't talk his way out of the mess I was in. He couldn't tell me not to worry. He couldn't give me a reason why this was happening and tell me it was ridiculous and a big mistake and that he'd get me out within the hour. The insecurity shook me, and I found myself pushing him off the pedestal where I had positioned him for the longest time.

Depressed, I started to evaluate my life. During this time, my mother, a strong Christian woman who was a faithful prayer warrior, kept telling me to have faith. "God will use this experience," she said. Sure, I had faith, but I also had a lot of questions.

What am I doing, living this kind of life?

What does the future hold?

What am I sacrificing for my family?

Did I sign up for this?

If God was in the middle of orchestrating a brilliant plan, I couldn't see it. But my mother could, and she continued to encourage me to pray. To believe. To trust God. And in more small ways than big, I started allowing Him to move in me and change me in ways only He could. One step at a time.

2

Knights of the City

Far from the world of that gray prison, and years earlier, I was a young woman with stars in my eyes. My childhood dream of being a dancer was coming true, and it would lead me right into the arms of my future husband. A friend of mine tipped me off to a local dance company that was holding auditions. Jeff Kutash, a former Golden Gloves boxer who was doing choreography for TV shows, movies, and Vegas performances, had a local dancing company called Dancin' Machine. They were known for bringing street dancing to the public in the early '70s and '80s.

I auditioned for the troupe in 1983. I was doubtful I'd get in. About thirty men and women flitted around the dance studio, sporting gaudy 1980s garb—neon leg warmers, colorful headbands, shiny leggings. Some were stretching their long, lean limbs, and others were coolly mingling with one another, oozing unmistakable confidence.

The competition was fierce. Quickly doing a once-over across the room, I saw seasoned dancers. Experienced dancers. Dancers who had studied hard, rehearsed long, and knew what they were doing. They could gracefully transition from a break-dancing move to a triple pirouette and then tap their hearts out. I was impressed and, I'll admit, intimidated.

I filled out the audition form and got my number. After an hour or so, we were taught the choreography for several songs, including "Stayin' Alive" and "Far from Over." We practiced the entire afternoon until we were ready to give our final performance in front of the dancing company's judges. Needless to say, it was a nerve-racking moment, but I didn't let my anxiety get the best of me. I gave it my all.

At the end of the day, we all lined up near the back of the studio and waited in hopeful anticipation for our numbers to be called. Mine was the last one Jeff barked out. I was shocked. Sure, I was confident I had natural talent, but I lacked the technique and extensive professional training the other dancers had.

Jeff approached me as I was ready to leave. He was always so encouraging. "Listen, Camille," he said. "I know you're not as trained as the other girls, but you're special. I see something different in you. People notice you when you dance. Just work real hard, take extra classes when you can, and come to all the rehearsals." He smiled and mussed my hair in an affectionate, fatherly gesture. "You'll do fine. I know you will."

I was so excited I could barely stand it.

That night I went to bed and I imagined my future. There would be dancing. Lots of dancing. Dancing around the world. Dancing on Broadway. I'd dance across the stage in front of thousands of people who came just to see me. Whenever I daydreamed, I never thought about falling in love.

I was only in the troupe a couple of months when Jeff was hired by movie producer Michael Franzese to choreograph a film for him in Florida. *Knights of the City*, originally named *Cry of the City* during the shooting, was a dance musical about a street gang trying to get a record deal. It was released in 1986 and starred Leon Isaac Kennedy, who also wrote the script, and Janine Turner, who would later become a household name for her role on *Northern Exposure*. Sammy Davis Jr. had a cameo appearance, and the Fat Boys performed a dance/rap number.

Jeff had already hired twelve dancers from the company to work in the picture. I was not on his list. I was friends with a couple of the dancers, though, and rumor had it that there were plenty of dancing opportunities in that part of Florida at various nightclubs. One of my girlfriends suggested, "Just come down to Miami and I'll hook you up with this guy named Mohammed. He's got a smokin' nightclub, and he's always hiring dancers. It's the real deal, and they put on great shows." Mohammed's club was a Miami hot spot. Three times the size of the Pachuco—a twenty-one-and-under club in the City of Industry—with multiple floors and a dazzling light show, it was the place to be on the weekends.

Sometime in February 1984, I dipped into my savings and bought a one-way plane ticket for a hundred bucks. I shared the news with my parents—I was leaving California. As expected, my mom warned me to be careful, and though I knew she didn't approve of my plans wholeheartedly, she was never one to forbid me to do anything. She never discouraged me from pursuing my dancing career, but I always got a lecture on the dangers of being tempted by the pressures of the entertainment industry. My dad's script was the same. "Go for it. I'm proud of you. Explore the world and experience new things. Work hard—and be good."

I didn't know until Michael told me years later, but when I was hired as a dancer for the movie, my dad called him and told him I was a little green in the film industry. He wanted Michael's guarantee that the production was legit and that there was—and would be—no funny business going on with his daughter.

The conversation took place before Michael and I had officially met. I would have been mortified had I known about the phone call. My dad's fatherly warnings and concern sparked a strong curiosity in Michael about me. It made him wonder, *Who is this girl?* and developed in him a genuine desire to make sure I was taken care of and didn't get into any kind of trouble.

I ended up doing one show at Mohammed's club before visiting the film set to see what was going on. The dancing community was always hungry for any kind of work. They'd show up on movie sets all the time to see if extras or backup dancers were needed. Dancers would play just about any role to get some work, even if it meant waving a flag around in a thirty-second appearance on camera.

Knights of the City was being filmed in different locations all over southern Florida. There were sets at the Sound Stage in Hollywood, Miami, and Fort Lauderdale. I don't remember which set I walked on. I do specifically remember not going on the set to purposely run into Jeff. I simply was bit by the curiosity bug. I'd never seen the behind-the-scenes life of a movie. I wondered what it was like, and I had the perfect opportunity to satisfy my interest. It didn't take long for me to run into Jeff, though.

He looked happy to see me. "Hey, Cammy!" he shouted, surrounded by a handful of dancers. "What are you doing here?"

I gave him a big hug. "Oh, a dancer friend of mine invited me down to check out the film and see what's going on."

"Well, as it turns out, I need to replace a couple of my dancers, so . . ." He grinned. "How would you feel about getting a part in the movie?"

Wow! This dream-come-true stuff is never ending!

Jeff made the arrangements, and I stayed with a few girls who were leaving the set in a few days, at the Marina Bay Club. All the elite dancers and major actresses were staying on the same floor. I couldn't believe I got so lucky. Little did I know, Michael had something to do with the cozy arrangement, based on my dad's phone call to him. He wanted me where he could keep an eye on me.

Dorian Sanchez was one of my roommates who were on their way off set. She had just picked up a role in the popular film *Dirty Dancing*; today she is one of the disco choreographers for the hit TV series *So You Think You Can Dance?* I was in the big leagues now. This small-town Mexican girl was hobnobbing with professional actors and dancers who had been in the business for a long time. It was a dream come true.

My role in the film was playing one of "Jasmine's Girls," and I shot about three dance scenes. When I went to wardrobe to pick up my costume, I couldn't stop laughing. I just happened to get the boldest and brightest outfit of all the girls. The shiny, turquoise Lycra leggings were coupled with a turquoise leopard-print leotard. I thought it looked ridiculous, but all of Jasmine's girls wore similar eye-catching costumes. When I saw myself on film, I was surprisingly impressed. The wardrobe director made a good choice because it was hard not to miss us girls in our garish outfits.

Being on the set was a blast. Aside from grueling workouts, rehearsals, and shooting schedules, we usually had a few hours during the week to relax. There was at least one party going on every night. Someone was always celebrating something or throwing a bash just because. I didn't attend many of those soirees because I kept to myself and took what Jeff had told me months ago to heart. "Work hard. Rehearse a lot. Keep improving." I felt I had been given the chance of a lifetime to dance, and I didn't want to screw it up by getting caught up in the social scene. I wanted to be known by the production staff and crew as a great dancer and a hard worker.

Dancers are wonderful to hang out with. They're laid-back and free-spirited. And dancing is a part of who they are. They dance every chance they get. There were always dance-offs and impromptu challenges. While most of the dancers were friendly and good-natured off set, they were brutal on the dance floor. Competition was ferocious, and everyone wanted to get noticed. Blonde, beautiful, and extremely talented, Katie was one of the few dancers I connected with. We still keep in touch.

When we met, she was always gushing about Michael this and Michael that. She talked about this Michael character with a dreamy look in her eye. I wondered if it was the same Michael all the other women on the set were talking about. *It must be,* I thought. Since arriving I'd heard the gossip about the executive producer, Michael Franzese. He was a single, successful, handsome, and—get this—super-nice eligible bachelor who treated everyone with kindness and respect. Katie asked if I'd met him yet. I shrugged my shoulders. "No, but I'm sure I'll probably see him around."

What is the big deal? I wondered. *Who is this mystery Michael guy? What's all the fuss about? What's so great about him?*

I was about to find out.

One afternoon all the dancers were hanging out by the pool. I had been on location for a couple of weeks and was grateful for some leisure time. My body was sore from rehearsing. I knew a swim and relaxing in the Florida sun would do the trick and cure my dancing aches and pains.

It was an amazing day. The sun was shining. There wasn't a cloud in sight. The sounds of splashing, horseplay, and laughter permeated the air, meshing perfectly with the salsa music that was blaring from a poolside stereo. The mood almost reminded me of home, of the lively neighborhood kids flooding our driveway with their boom boxes and dance moves. It was a lighthearted but intense energy.

I recognized Michael sitting at a table with a couple of his friends I had seen around the set. He was an attractive man with thick, jet-black hair and a prominent Roman nose. His strong jaw line accentuated his masculinity, but his smile softened the rough edge. Casting director David Wilder rounded out the table.

I had just come out of the pool and, while standing in the hot sun, grabbed the ends of my hair to squeeze the excess water out of them. When I opened my eyes, I caught a glimpse of Michael staring at me. He wasn't leering in a creepy kind of way, but his gaze made me feel awkward, as if all his attention was focused on me. My eyes met his for few seconds, and I quickly walked over to where my friend Carol was lounging.

A few minutes later, I noticed a ton of commotion going on around Michael's table. There were bags of Danskin and Capezio merchandise piled in a massive heap around David's assistant. She was handing out what looked like a bunch of free stuff. Her arms were loaded with brightly colored leg warmers, leotards, and head-bands. The girls were going nuts. It was worse than the epic Barneys Warehouse Sale.

Michael was the source behind the generous giveaways. As I toweled myself off, all I could hear were the dancers running up to him and gushing, "Thank you, Michael! Thank you sooo much." I thought it was all a bit much. Not the freebies, but how they fla-grantly vied for his attention. I couldn't imagine how he could tell one desperate girl from the next. They all mimicked the same routine: compliment him, subtly touch his arm or hand, bat their eyelashes, stick out their well-endowed body parts, and purr sweet nothings in his ear.

When Carol and I finally walked over to the mayhem, hop-ing to get a few handouts, the assistant stood empty-handed. She looked at us apologetically and said, "Sorry, girls. I got nothing left." *No matter*, I thought and went back to lounging. I quickly forgot all about the free stuff as the hot sun poured over my body, reminding me of the golden rays back home. I felt homesick.

Suddenly, I felt a presence disturb my relaxation and block the sun. I opened my eyes and sat up. I couldn't tell who was standing in front of me because even in light of the mysterious shadow, the sun's glare was so powerful. As I shielded my face with my hand, my eyes met the smile of the famous Michael Franzese looming over me, with David by his side. It was the first encounter we ever had. I wasn't surprised or excited to see him so close. I felt indifferent. And frankly, I was a little bored of the hoopla surrounding him, and I certainly didn't want to get caught up in it.

David grabbed a lounge chair and dragged it closer to mine. "Hi, Camille. I want to introduce you to Michael Franzese. He's the executive producer of the film."

He turned to Michael, who had the biggest grin on his face, and said, "And this, Michael, is Camille Garcia."

"Hi, Camille," Michael warmly greeted me. His dark eyes pierced into mine. They were gentle, calm, almost sweet. I was caught off guard by his amiable demeanor. His mannerisms made me feel comfortable, as if I'd known him a long time. I think that's one of Michael's gifts. He can make even a stranger feel right at home.

"I noticed you didn't get any of the promotion merchandise we were giving out. I'm so sorry about that." He bent down and picked up about five bags exploding with more leg warmers and T-shirts than I would ever know what to do with.

My mouth dropped. "Oh, my goodness. Thank you so much. But seriously, it's too much. I can't take it all."

Michael winked and laughed. "Well, what am I going to do with all these girlie things? Have you seen what I look like in a pair of leg warmers?" He was so charming it was hard not to enjoy his company. I thanked him, and he said, "Nice to meet you, Camille. I'm sure I'll see you around."

So there I was, on a plastic lounge chair, covered up to my eyeballs in bags of dancewear. I felt a bit sheepish, so I started handing out the items to Carol and some of the other dancers who didn't get anything last time. Some of the girls noticed the exchange between Michael and me, and their faces came alive with curiosity. No one said a word to me, but I did notice the woman who had originally handed out the clothing shoot a disapproving glance in my direction. I guess she wasn't too happy I got more stuff than she was told to hand out.

I saw Michael again the following week. It wasn't one of my finest moments. I had just gotten out of the shower and had finished writing a letter to my old boyfriend Eddie. I wanted to see how he was doing and tell him what I was up to. I headed down to the hotel lobby to mail the letter and was looking forward to a good night's sleep in my warm, cozy bed. My dripping-wet hair was plastered to my makeup-free face, and I wore my signature casual outfit, a bright-orange oversized dress that buttoned down the front. It wasn't the most stylish thing I owned, but I didn't care. It was comfortable.

As I approached the mail slot, I happened to see Michael walk in with a drop-dead-gorgeous brunette by his side. I guessed she was his wife or girlfriend. They were enjoying each other's company, smiling and laughing with each step. A connection was obvious. *Figures. Of course he'd be attached to a supermodel.* Michael immediately noticed me and nodded in my direction.

As I opened the mail slot to dump in the envelope, I felt someone grab my arm. I was startled until I realized it was Michael. He broke out into a mischievously adorable smile and said, "You don't really want to mail that, do you?"

"What? Of course I do. Trust me. I need to mail it."

He drew in a little closer and playfully shook his head. "No. I don't think you do."

I laughed. I knew there was some kind of flirting going on, but it felt awkward as this stunning woman stood only a few feet away from us. I decided to bring up the elephant in the room. I pointed toward the supermodel. "Isn't that your girlfriend?"

"Joanne? Oh no!" Michael seemed embarrassed about the misunderstanding. "No, Joanne is actually my best friend's girlfriend, who just flew into town. She has a small part in the film, and I told my buddy I'd pick her up and show her the ropes."

"Oh." And with that clarification, we both looked at each other and said, "Okay, well, I'll see you around."

I saw Michael around the set a few more times, and more innocent flirting ensued. He would casually invite me to all kinds of parties and events, but I declined most of them. It's funny. He claims I stood him up five times, but I never officially accepted most of those invitations. I always threw out a casual, "I'll see." I wasn't trying to be difficult; I was just being overly cautious. I didn't know Michael from Adam, and it didn't matter to me that he was a bigwig on the set. All I knew was that every girl wanted him, and I didn't want to be just another girl.

Michael's hotel room happened to be diagonal from mine, so I could see all the activity in and out of his room. Girls were always floundering around his door. Dancers made a point of practicing their routines in the hallway, showing off their slender physiques and sensual moves in front of their favorite audience of one. On occasion, I even saw a handful of Playmates coming in and out of his room. Girls flocked to the guy.

One day my friend Katie knocked on my door and told me Michael was having a get-together in his room. She begged me to go with her. "Come on, Camille. Let's go say hi." Like the slew of other women on the set, she still had an unabating crush on Michael. Katie hoped he could help her with her career, as she was a well-known dancer in the industry, and he had oodles of connections.

She wasn't bothered by the competition, and, truthfully, I admired her confidence.

At that point, however, Michael's room was the last place I wanted to spend the night. "Katie, you go," I tried to coax her. "Have a good time. I'm gonna take a shower and clean up, and when I'm done, if there are people still there, I'll stop by. I promise." Persistent Katie didn't take no for an answer, and practically dragged me out of the room. I was wearing my orange T-shirt dress. What a shocker.

A pay-per-view boxing match was showing on a big-screen TV in Michael's room, and people were milling around in every corner of his massive suite. I wondered where the man of the hour was, and then I saw him surrounded by ten or so men and women who appeared to be fawning over him. He had a large black towel draped over his shoulders and was getting his hair trimmed. *How pretentious,* I thought, and looked away, rolling my eyes. I looked back, out of sheer curiosity, and noticed a woman scrubbing his hands. He was also getting a manicure. *What is this? A Michael Franzese spa day?*

As soon as Michael saw us, he greeted us in his gracious way: "Camille! Katie! How are you, girls?" It was strange. As important and grandiose as he looked getting primped by professionals at his own soiree, he was refreshingly friendly and personable. He always made a deliberate effort to acknowledge and talk to you whenever you walked in a room. I liked that about him.

Katie and I walked over, and he asked us about our day, the rehearsals, whether or not we were tired or ready to start filming. At some point, Katie had to leave to talk to someone else, and Michael and I spent some time together. As we were shooting the breeze, he called over his best bud, Frankie. The two of them were attached at the hip and went everywhere together.

"Frankie! I want you to meet someone." Frankie walked over to me and extended his hand. He was a short, thin man with a receding hairline. Though not the best looking guy in the room, he was charming, especially with his thick New York accent.

"Frankie, this is Camille."

"Nice to meet you."

"Here, come sit down and talk with us," Michael said.

Before I left, he invited me to stop by again a few days later. I gave him my routine ambiguous answer of "Maybe," and never showed up. It was obvious Michael had some interest in me, but I wasn't sure how much. I kept cool and continued to keep a comfortable distance. One time he asked me to meet him at the pool bar (for milk and cookies, he suggested, since I didn't drink), and though I had agreed to see him, I was stuck in rehearsal until one in the morning. Another rendezvous that didn't happen.

I didn't share with anyone the amount of attention Michael was lavishing my way. Not even with my friend Katie. I called my mom one night, however, to get her perspective. She was so happy to hear my voice and kept telling me how much she missed and loved me.

"Mom, I think the producer of the film might be interested in me."

She paused for a second. "Might be? Come on, Camille. You know if he's interested in you or not. So how old is he, anyway?"

"I don't know. I never asked him. But he's definitely not a boy, and he's definitely older than me." Michael was thirty-two, twelve years older than me.

After a few more motherly questions, my mom, in classic prayer-warrior fashion, said, "Okay, I'll pray for you that you're careful and you make the right decisions, and that everything will work out between you two as it's supposed to. And I'm going to pray for Michael."

"Mom! Why on earth would you pray for Michael?"

"Because I don't even know him, Cammy. And it sounds like you don't really either. I'm going to pray that God guides him in his intentions and ways with you." My mom left me with this important lesson—pray. Pray for your husband. Pray for your kids. Pray for your family. And pray always. I hope I instill this practice in my kids with as much passion as my mom did in me.

Mom had a lot of practice praying for our family, especially her husband. All his life he was feeding and clothing the homeless, raising funds for this or that project, and marching for some cause or political organization. And all the while we were getting yet another eviction notice slapped on our front door, and one dinnertime after another came and left without anything for the Garcia kids to eat. It was like he was trying to save the world but forgot about his own family.

When my mother passed away from breast cancer in 2001, a lot of buried feelings resurfaced. I was bitter. I thought he should have treated her better. He should have provided for her more. He should have been more appreciative of what a great woman, wife, and mother she was. I knew I had to stop the complaining, though; it would have disappointed my mom. She didn't raise me to spew such venom.

After she gave her life to the Lord, she never said a bad thing about my dad, nor was she outwardly angry with him because of the dumb things he did. And Lord knows, there was a lot she could have said. Instead, my mom kept her mouth shut and loved on him, prayed for him, and stuck it out because that was the commitment she made when she married him.

I felt bad for my mom. When I was a freshman in high school, my dad's drunken antics were becoming commonplace. Instead of him acting out two or three times a month, he was acting out every weekend. There was a certain point in her life when I could see her becoming affected by the drama. She changed. Her eyes got heavy. She seemed depressed. She moped around, unsmiling. She was tired instead of her usual chipper self. I was worried.

I knew something had to give, but I didn't know what. I knew my mother would never leave her husband. She tried it once. I was in elementary school, and my mom needed some space from Dad. She gathered her kids, packed up the car, and drove to San Diego to spend time with my grandmother, "Nana." We were greeted with open arms, mainly because my grandmother hoped my mom had come to her senses and was finally going to leave him.

Nana and my mom's siblings did some pretty persuasive talking and tried to convince Mom to stay indefinitely. It was time for her to start a new life, they said. She could have a whole new future. A better future. For her and the kids. It was an option, but I don't know how serious my mom took the suggestion. We stayed there for a few weeks.

At home by himself, my father blew a gasket. He came to see us every weekend and pouted, hemmed and hawed, and begged my mom to come back. She was quiet and gave him no response. It looked like she was going to stay put for a while. The last weekend he came, my father basically ignored my mother's silence. He showed up with his brothers in a pickup truck, barged into our new apartment (that we got with the help of Mom's family), and started loading the truck up with our belongings.

"Irma," he yelled as he carried a stack of boxes out the house, "this is ridiculous. We're a family. We are not living apart. I'm going to change. I promise. Things are going to be different. But you have to come home. You need to be home." So we packed up and left and came back to Norwalk.

That was the last straw for my mom's family. They had given us a little bit of cash, helped us find a place to stay, even registered us for school, and now Mom, at least in their eyes, had slapped them in the face. *Thanks, but no thanks* was how they interpreted her departure.

But my mother's rationale for going back to her husband was not out of spite. She wasn't trying to hurt her mom or her siblings. She wanted us to be a family. She had seen the irreparable damage that comes from divorce and didn't want us to go through it. She thought it was better to carry some wounds from our dysfunction than to bear lasting scars from a broken marriage. And in many ways, as sick or twisted as it may sound, she was right.

I also think she didn't want to be reliant on her family. She didn't want to feel owned by them. She hated them doing her favors only if she agreed to live her life the way they wanted her to. They would do X only if she would do Y. My mom would rather live with the choice she made and never ask her family for a cent or for help of any kind than to be chained by their expectations or their money.

What ended up changing my mom's life ironically changed the course of her family's life. She found Jesus. But first she met Peggy.

Peggy was married to a well-connected politician named Robert, who also happened to be a close friend of my dad's. She was sweet, kind, and radiated a simple beauty. She didn't turn many heads, unlike her handsome husband, who, we all knew, was having a little more fun on the side than he should have. The closer my mom got to Peggy, the more encouraged she became. The melancholy in her eyes was replaced by a glimmer of hope.

Peggy was a great influence on my mom because she was always positive and dealt with life with a smile on her face. And not a fake smile either. She was a gracious woman and a caring host, but more important, she was genuine. She lived her life more from her heart than from the lofty standards of how a politician's wife should live. Peggy's solution to everything was to pray. Whatever the problem, there was an answer in prayer. My mother sensed there was something more in Peggy's life than the power of positive thinking. She was right.

Mom had been taking us to mass at St. John of God every Sunday. She wholeheartedly believed in God, but she'd never had a personal relationship with Him. After attending services with Peggy at her church, my mom changed. When she became a Christian, she told me she felt a difference. Her faith became even more alive. She felt more peaceful even though her life was still in shambles.

My mom always had a meek and mild character, but I did witness some painful outbursts and crying fits. I remember when our family had plans to go out to dinner. It was a big deal to eat at Curly Jones, so my little brother Dino and I took our baths and sat out by the curb, waiting for my dad to show up. What we didn't know was that it was payday. Every time a car passed that looked like my dad's, Dino and I yelled out, "Daddy! Daddy!" It seemed as if every other car bore a striking resemblance to our station wagon.

My mother heard the commotion from inside the house. She got so angry at us, but at the time we couldn't figure out why; we were just waiting for our dad to come home. When night fell, she grabbed both of us by our shirts. Her eyes were puffy and her face bright red. "Don't you get it? Your father is not coming home. We are not going anywhere. Now, get back inside the house!" That night we each were punished with a painful spanking. It was unfair. We were just waiting for Daddy.

After my mother's conversion, incidents like that never happened again. Her attitude completely shifted. She was less worried about the future and what her husband was or was not doing. If there was ever a living testament to the power of Jesus in one's life, it was my mother. She started handling her pain and angst in a different way, a better way. I admired her for it because I knew it wasn't easy. I might have been young, but I was no dummy. I knew things were tough for my mom. But she bore her burden with grace and a character that could only be shaped by and infused with the power of the Holy Spirit.

She once told me, "Cammy, I now know what my purpose is: not to divorce my husband, not to be angry with him in front of you children, and not to cause any more chaos. I'm supposed to be the light in the house of darkness." When her spiritual life changed, she started preaching in her loving way about choices even more. She reminded us kids that no matter how bleak her life may have looked, she made a choice every day to be happy.

"This is my life," she would tell me. "I made the choice to marry your father, and I made the choice to be a mother of seven children. I need to make the choice to be the best wife and mother I can be. Even when I don't feel happy, I still choose every morning to be positive."

My mom's connection with the Holy Spirit was evident, and her prayer life became charged. When she gave her life over to God, she started sensing a deep-rooted darkness in the house. She knew it was the alcoholism that held my dad captive. She prayed against it with a remarkable faithfulness, without ceasing and always believing that God would hear her. She prayed so much my dad would break out in long-winded rants about how she was going nuts because of this crazy religion nonsense. But there were other times I know in my heart he appreciated it. Who wouldn't be grateful for much-needed prayers when your household is falling apart?

My mom spent the rest of her life with my dad in a quiet assurance that everything would work out and he would one day change, if only by the grace of God. There were times I'd get frustrated and say, "Mom, can't you just complain and be normal?" But she wouldn't. She refused. She made a decision to live the right way. A kind way. A way that showed grace, was stable, and was unconditionally loving.

"What good would it have done if I'd gotten angry, Camille?" she replied whenever I questioned her devotion to my dad. "It would have been even worse for you kids. You know that." Again, she was right.

I became a Christian at the same time my mom did. I didn't do it because of what my mom shared with me about Jesus or the Bible. I didn't do it because Peggy also talked to me about what it meant. I decided to give my life to the Lord because of the change I saw in my mom. It was real. It was genuine. And it was something that I wanted.

My uncle Alfred had died around the same time as my conversion. It was a sad juncture in my life and one in which I asked many questions. *Is there really a God? Is there a heaven? What happens when we die? What is life for?* I didn't find those answers immediately after I prayed for my salvation, but I did find peace of mind. I've found that peace is much better than having the luxury of answers.

Even as a thirteen-year-old girl, I felt the Holy Spirit working in my life to help me make good decisions. I wasn't perfect by any means, but I believe that with God's help I had a better high school and college experience than I would have had without His guidance and inner workings.

I am eternally grateful to my mother for giving us the gift of faith. Her commitment to God, her children, and her husband left a legacy for me to live by. Time and time again, she taught me that life is never easy. It's tough, but you get through it. And she reminded me of the sacred vows of marriage. Sure, it's easy to get divorced and run away when relationships break down and the fairy tale disappears, but God expects us to give a hundred percent in our marriages. "To have and to hold" for a lifetime is serious business, not mere words that seem to have lost their meaning over the years and that couples sometimes mindlessly recite.

And later, when my marriage to Michael blew up in ways I could never have imagined in my wildest dreams, I was reminded of my mother's wisdom: "Pray and hang in there. God will show up. He always does."

My life was so exciting in those days when Michael and I were just getting to know each other, but I would quickly be leaning on Mom's wise words, and much sooner than I could imagine.

My beautiful parents.

Me at twelve years old,
Hollenback Park, East LA.

Me at eighteen, a year before I met Mike.

3

Who Is Michael Franzese?

A few days later, Jeff announced that Michael and the rest of the head honchos from the film were stopping by the dance studio to watch us rehearse. They wanted to see our numbers and make sure they were clean and ready for filming. You can't even imagine the buzz of excitement that flooded the air. The girls were freaking out. "He's coming! He's coming! Michael is going to be watching us!" There was a whole lot of beautifying going on that afternoon.

It's funny. Michael was the biggest woman magnet I'd ever known. Even after filming was over and we were officially an item, women were still hot on his trail. I remember being at his office in California and answering his telephone, only to discover that a good portion of the incoming calls were from dancers and actresses from the film, looking to talk to him.

That day, Jeff was his usual drill-sergeant self, barking orders at us to tighten our routine. It seemed he got his point across best by yelling at us and using colorful language. "WHAT ARE YOU GUYS *doing*?" he'd scream. "What is this? This isn't dancing. I don't know what it is. But it's definitely not dancing. STOP WASTING MY TIME; START SHOWING ME WHAT WE'RE PAYING YOU TO DO!"

When Michael walked in with his entourage, Jeff broke into a smile. "Almost ready for you guys. You're gonna love the show we put on for you." The group took a seat on a bench right in front of the dance floor. After a brief introduction, Jeff yelled out the numbers and we ran through our group performances, pushing our bodies, our minds, and everything we learned in rehearsal to the limit.

The minute he called out, "Jasmine's Bad Girls," my stomach churned. My palms were sweaty, and there was a slight flurry of butterflies in my stomach. I was nervous and also intimidated. I was one of the least-experienced dancers on the set, and I wanted to make a good impression on the people running the show. Michael and his crew were only a handful of feet from where we danced. I highly doubt they were judging our technique and skill. When a group of men watch a bunch of beautiful dancers moving seductively in supertight clothes, believe you me, they're not trying to figure out where the girls need some improvement in their performance.

As I danced, I noticed Michael kept his eyes on me. He even smiled a couple of times. When I sprinted to the back to watch the other numbers, his stare followed. I wouldn't have known if it hadn't been for one of the girls who pulled me aside and loudly whispered, "Cammy, Michael totally has the hots for you! He keeps looking at you."

I shook my head. "No, that's silly. I'm sure he was looking at you."

"What are you, blind? Girl, he's practically boring holes in your head!" When I finally admitted to myself that it could be possible, my reaction startled me. I found myself getting a little giddy from the attention. I couldn't believe it. I was starting to privately enjoy Michael's spotlight.

When we were finished, the dancers were milling around the studio, making plans for the evening. I saw my friend Karen, who had a starring role in the film, talking to Michael. When she noticed me, she called out, "Hey Camille, are you coming out with us to the nightclub tonight?" I was about to give my customary answer, "No," when Michael motioned for me to come over.

Karen turned to Michael and said, "You can bring someone if you want."

Out of nowhere, I blurted out. "He is. He's bringing me." Michael seemed pleasantly startled. It was the first bold move I'd made since we were introduced. I gave him a million-dollar smile and intertwined my arm with his. It was subtle proof to him that, "*Yes, Michael Franzese, I like you, too.*"

For the first time since our missed "dates," I made an appearance at the club that evening. A famous '80s band was playing, and all of Michael's friends were there. I was having a blast and didn't even notice that it was already midnight. Michael still hadn't shown up. By that point, I was certain he wasn't going to stop by, but at least he wouldn't be able to accuse me of standing him up.

I sat next to Michael's friend Pete, who didn't hide the fact that he liked me. He focused all his attention on me and was a little too close for comfort, but because he wasn't being brash or intrusive, it didn't bother me. The cacophony of the blaring music and the mishmash of different conversations going on at once made it hard to hear what Pete was saying. I found myself spending much of the evening nodding and smiling.

At midnight, I saw a dark and handsome man head toward our U-shaped table. My heart skipped a beat. As soon as the crew noticed his arrival, everyone started making the routine fuss. "Hey, Mike, sit here." "What are you drinking?" "Come and dance with me." I was getting used to people making a big stink whenever Michael showed up. He said his hellos, and it only took a few minutes for him to whisk himself over to my side. "Hi, Camille. It's good to finally see you," he joked, with a twinkle in his eye. "How are you?"

He quickly motioned for Pete to move over so he could sit in Pete's spot. Pete let out a groan and balked at the request, but once Michael gave him a gimme-a-break-just-move-over-will-ya? look, Pete sighed and said, "Michael, why don't you sit here?" Michael and I spent the rest of the night captivated by each other, indulging in carefree conversation in our own little world while the nightclub spun in chaos around us. We talked for hours, oblivious of the twenty other people around us. Oblivious of the rhythmic, pulse-pounding music. Oblivious even of the time.

Michael apologized for being late. He told me he had been asleep and had asked Frankie to call and wake him up only if I was at the nightclub. He was so tired that he didn't want to risk a night out if I wasn't there. I thought it was so sweet, but I also felt bad. I put a hand on his knee and said, "If you were really tired, you could have seen me another night, you know."

Michael laughed. "Where? In my dreams? No way! I wanted to see you."

After that rendezvous, which lasted until the wee hours of the morning, our dates became more frequent. We had dinner a few times the following week. The more I talked to Michael, the more I liked him. He was a nice guy, always respectful and cordial. He never pressured me to take our friendship to a physical level. There were no visible neon signs or red flags that made me question moving the relationship forward. Oh sure, Michael was a lot older than the guys I had dated before, but so what? I wanted a mature man.

The biggest problem I had was with the rumor mill around the set. Gossip was spreading like wildfire about what Michael and I were up to. Many girls came up to me with warnings to stay away from him. Some may have come from a place of genuine concern, but I don't believe most of the comments were sincere. This one told me to "be careful." That one told me, "Michael's sleeping with other women." One dancer gave me the heads-up that another dancer, who had just left the set and was in my dancing company, had a big crush on him and was using her "sources" to keep an eye on me. This woman had been in the company for a long time and had a lot of connections; in so many words, I was warned, *If you know what's good for you and your dancing, you'll stay away from Michael.*

The different forms of threats to "lay off" were what kept me pacing our relationship at an almost glacial speed. I didn't want people to get the wrong idea. The problem was, on a movie set, where your life consists of practicing, rehearsing, and filming nonstop, there isn't much else to do except gossip. It was a hot pastime.

I remember when Todd Bridges, the famous actor from *Diff'rent Strokes*, came to visit our set. I met him at the pool, and we struck up a conversation. The next day, the buzz was that Todd and I were dating. The rumor came out of left field. It was ridiculous. Matter of fact, I remember talking to him about his girlfriend the whole time. It bothered me how people were quick to whisper lies and cause problems, making up stories about things that weren't true. Didn't they have anything better to do?

I also heard a lot of mean stuff that started to come out about Michael and me. All the hearsay fell along the lines of, "Camille is using Michael" or "Michael is using Camille." I was somewhat offended and even hurt by these rumors, but my advocate, Joanne, the stunning girlfriend of one of Michael's best friends, reminded me to pay no mind to the silliness. "Listen, Camille. If you can see yourself in a relationship with Michael and you really like him, why do you care what people say? Forget them. They're just jealous. If you want to go for it and see what happens, go for it."

I knew she was right, but I didn't jump in publicly with the news of our togetherness too quick. When Michael and I were officially a couple (which basically just happened; there was nothing official about it), I still made a noble effort to keep things as quiet as possible. If we went out to dinner, I never let him pick me up. I would walk to the tennis courts and meet him there. I tried to avoid making public appearances with him as much as possible.

Michael hated the secrecy. He thought it was unnecessary and a waste of energy, but I begged him to follow along just for me. No matter how frustrated he got, however, he always respected my wishes. "Okay, Camille, however you want me to do this, I'll do it."

It only took a few days for me to give up my ridiculous hiding strategies for good. Michael invited me to his house in Del Ray. We ordered some take-out and spent the night eating, talking, and watching movies. It was a quiet, intimate evening. Michael sat on his oversized couch, and I sprawled out below him on the floor, enjoying the way he gently massaged my neck and played with my hair.

I felt pretty tired and took a look at my watch, disappointed by how late it was. The evening had flown by. I got up and stretched my legs. Yawning, I said, "Michael, I've got to go. It's getting late."

He wasn't about to let me go that easily. "Cam, it's a big house. There are five bedrooms you can choose to stay in. Spend the night here. Get some rest."

Though I was confident he wasn't going to try anything, I was still cautious about the physical aspect of the relationship. I didn't want to rush into anything until I was absolutely ready. "No, I really need to go back."

Michael got up and cupped my face in his hands. His touch was warm and soothing. "Cam, you can trust me. You know that."

I felt terrible. "I do trust you. It's not that. I just need to go." I was also plagued with whispers from my mother back home. I kept hearing her say, "Camille, be careful. Do the right thing. Hang out with the right people. Be wise. Make good decisions." I didn't want to do anything I might regret, so I kept my stance.

Michael kissed me on the forehead and agreed to take me back to Fort Lauderdale. That night I realized that if I wanted to pursue this relationship and see where it would lead, I needed to be more open and not hide the fact that I liked him. Joanne was right. Who cared?

When filming came to a close two months later, our relationship was common knowledge. I felt a strange sense of relief. A weight had been lifted from my shoulders. Now I could focus on my dancing and Michael without any unnecessary distractions.

While I knew Michael had a lot of money, he wasn't ostentatious about it. His house in Del Ray was beautiful, for instance, but it wasn't extravagant. He didn't need to flaunt his more-than-comfortable lifestyle. A man of his caliber typically donned fancy Italian suits and Gucci loafers, but Michael was more comfortable in jeans and Top-Siders or Vans. He also drove a Cadillac, not a Ferrari or a Lamborghini. He didn't make an issue of having a lot of money, so it put less pressure on me and made me feel even more relaxed around him.

What took some getting used to was eating out. We always went to five-star restaurants, where the cheapest thing on the menu was a $30 hamburger. It was crazy. Who would spend that much money on one meal? I could live on thirty bucks for an entire week! Michael always noticed my hesitancy in ordering. I held on to the menu for dear life and stared at it longer than I needed to. I hated spending someone else's money for something so frivolous. But Michael paid no mind to my fuss. "Order whatever you want," he reassured me. "Trust me: you'll get used to ordering good food."

Though we spent a lot of time talking and getting to know each other, I never asked him too many personal questions, particularly about his past. My friend Katie had mentioned something to me about Michael still being married. "Everyone knows," she matter-of-factly said. I thought she was letting jealousy get the best of her.

I had always assumed Michael was divorced. I never thought to ask him about his marital status, because to me, it was obvious he wasn't married. He didn't wear a ring, made no mention of a wife, and was with me most of the time. We had just started dating, so I thought it was too soon to pry into his past. As our relationship grew and time went on, Michael did share that his divorce was final.

I know it's hard to believe, but I was never aware of his connection with organized crime. I knew he was an entrepreneur and owned a ton of property and car dealerships back home in New York. Michael told me that his father had some issues with the law, thus the frequent trips to New York to attend court hearings. I was under the impression that Sonny Franzese was in jail for conspiracy to rob a bank but was set up and therefore innocent. (Later I would find out Sonny was an underboss for the Colombo crime family and one of the most feared men in New York at one time.) The charges of conspiring to rob a bank didn't cause me to raise my eyebrows because, hey, my father was in and out of jail for petty stuff all the time. If anything, I understood how difficult that could be on a child, even an adult child. I also didn't associate Sonny's crimes with Michael. The problems and mistakes were his father's, not his. The son shouldn't have to pay for anything the father did wrong.

In a way I felt comfortable being with a man who had a father on the outs with the law. My father, Seferino Garcia, whom everyone called Fred, is a rebel at heart. A nonconformist who despised working for "the man," he is a Chicano activist who has spent his adult life fighting for the rights of farm workers, youth, and Hispanics in Los Angeles and Orange counties. When he was seventeen, he met civil rights activist and labor leader César Chávez. His life would never be the same again after meeting his hero. One of his greatest achievements was starting Barrio Carnalismo in 1972. This alliance, whose name, roughly translated, means "neighborhood of brothers," was a coalition of gang members, community leaders, and concerned parents whose mission was to promote peace in the community.

While my siblings and I were busy growing up, Dad fought to build community centers, create high school programs to educate young people about Hispanic culture, and lead neighborhood campaigns against violence. His driving force was bringing unity to our Chicano community. He was a likable guy and was friends with people from many different walks of life, including rival gang members. He had buddies in the Brown Berets, the Black Panthers, and the Crips.

Though genuinely good-natured, my dad had a very prominent rebellious side, and because of the questionable company he kept, he got in trouble with the law on many occasions. My mom was Fred's number one cheerleader, however. If it hadn't been for her always pulling for him and believing in what he was doing to promote unity and build a better community with Chicano pride (she even convinced him to register for classes at Cerritos College later on in his life), he would have ended up in prison or dead. My mom helped him make better choices, and I believe she even saved his life, although her support came with a hefty price tag.

When we kids were younger and before my dad committed most of his time and energy to these different volunteer projects, he was a steady provider. He worked at Mattel for a stint (we had the most toys in our neighborhood), Langley Aircraft, and General Motors for a few years. Once the activism took a core role in his life, though, the steady jobs stopped. And the money stopped. There were many nights my siblings and I sat and stared at an empty dinner table. My father also loved the bottle. He had a habit of collecting the little money he made and spending it on drinks with his homeboys.

My dad was a drinker and a fighter. It was part of his instinct. Growing up in a family with twenty-three kids, I imagine he needed to constantly be on guard in order to survive. And with a household of that size, how much attention—or food—can you get if you don't fight for it? I imagine not much.

True to his nature, my dad fought for what he wanted in the community. Sad thing is, I didn't think he put enough energy into fighting much for his kids or my mom when it came to providing for us. When the jobs stopped coming, he seemed ambivalent about feeding, clothing, and sheltering us. His attitude was, "My kids? Oh, they're fine. They're great kids. They do good in school. They play sports. They're popular. They're fine!" I believe my father truly thought we were fine. I don't think he purposely left us to fend for ourselves. And frankly, we were, for the most part, a pretty self-sufficient family.

But there were some harsh realities we dealt with. There were dozens of times when we went without electricity, food, or water. When, in a rare bout of luck, my Dad had a steady paycheck, he'd clock out at 5:00 on Friday and disappear until Monday. He'd return with empty pockets and reeking of the unmistakable stench of beer.

My mother, though calm and collected the majority of the time, would get ticked at him. He never understood why she got so upset that we didn't eat and had to sleep in the cold without any lights. "Irma," he'd question, "why the attitude? Our kids are fine. Everything is fine. So what if the lights were turned off last night? There was no harm done. And at least they had a roof over their heads. Isn't that what they really need?"

My dad, however, was far from fine. His drinking episodes colored our childhood and forced us to grow up rather quickly. There were many times before I had my license that I had to drive him home from somewhere because he was too drunk to drive. There were also many times he drove my siblings and me while drunk. He'd take what he called "shortcuts" and drive through people's lawns and parks. My uncles used to say that Fred had nine lives. I believe it's a miracle we made it out alive, especially my dad.

Being the oldest, I became adept at cleaning up his literal and figurative messes. When my dad would leave our house for the evening to go on a binge, I was never able to sleep. I'd wait up for him all night until I heard the distinctive creak of the front door opening and his signature stomps to let us know he was home. Those sounds roused me into defense and savior mode: get dad into the kitchen; quiet him down; find him something to eat; clean him up if he gets sick; get him on the couch; and pray that he would fall asleep.

As messed-up as my father's child rearing was, I never held a grudge (at least not for more than a few days). My mom made sure of this. Often she told me, "Don't blame your dad for what happened to us. It happened, and we can only move on. I made the choice to marry him, and I made the choice to stay with him."

Without a doubt, Mom was our rock and helped to shape our character in a godly way. She taught us how to survive through tough times. She taught us about commitment and how to grow close as a family. She taught us about forgiveness. Sure, the lessons were bred from a tough background, but I wouldn't trade my past (or my dad's crazy episodes) for what I learned and how it shaped me in my later years.

One time when I was around eleven, I had just fallen asleep, unsuccessfully waiting up for my dad, when I woke to a strange sound coming from the living room. It sounded like someone was playing darts. I turned into super daughter and started preparing for the drill. As I ran into the living room, I thought, *What am I going to feed him? We've got nothing to eat.*

I came to a screeching halt in the middle of the fiasco. I could not believe my eyes. Two young men from the neighborhood, in their early twenties, sat like zombies on the couch. Fear darkened their wide eyes, and their hands gripped the edge of the sofa so tight they were shaking. Over and over they whimpered, "Fred, what are you doing? You're scaring us. Stop it! Please, Fred, cut it out!"

My eyes turned toward the instigator, and I saw my dad, as cool as a cucumber, holding a bunch of dinner knives—we didn't own dinner knives, they were his private collection of blades that he kept under his bed—in his left hand. And then—*whoosh!*—a knife flew straight into the wall right above one of the guys' heads. The two panicked and continued begging, "Fred, stop it!" My dad ignored them and—*whoosh!*—another knife. This one landed inches from the last. His aim was getting worse. He was about to throw another knife when he noticed I was standing in the room.

His smile turned from suspicious to warm. "Skumpy!" My dad looked genuinely happy to see me. Whenever he used that nickname, he was always in a good mood.

"How you doing, Skumpy?" He motioned with his knife-holding hand to the guys on the couch, who looked like they were a few seconds shy of peeing their pants. "Come meet my homeboys."

I froze. I didn't know what to do. Drunk plus deadly weapons equals nothing good. Finally, I stammered, "D-d-dad, what are you doing?"

Whoosh. Another knife narrowly missed one of the guys' thick manes of dark hair. "Freeed," the poor sucker wailed. My dad hushed him up, "Shh! Stop whining. Don't move!"

At first, I had thought these homeboys were pretty stupid. Why didn't they just move? Then I realized they were scared to death of Fred and his brothers. Everyone knew the Garcia boys, and they also knew to stay away, because God only knew what they were capable of. These guys weren't so stupid after all.

"Dad," I pleaded, this time putting more volume in my voice and carefully enunciating each word. "What—are—you—*doing?*"

"Skumpy, relax. Me and the homeboys are having a little fun."

"Um, Dad. Throwing knives is definitely not fun. Cut it out. C'mon. It's time to go to bed." I wasn't talking to my dad to get him to stop; I knew he'd stop when he was good and ready. I was merely trying to distract him so his buddies could get off the couch and make a dash for the front door. I tried to give them "the eye" so they would catch on to my strategy, but they didn't budge. They were frozen to the couch, still whining and moaning.

"Look, Dad, stop!" This time I meant business. My dad looked at me and put his hands down, but not as an act of surrender; he looked like he'd had enough. The knife-throwing fest was beginning to lose its appeal. I turned to his homeboys and, in my best grown-up-listen-to-me-when-I'm-talking-to-you voice, said, "You guys get out of here now! Go home!" They hightailed it out of the house in a flash.

The house was quiet. It was just Dad and me. I was visibly annoyed, but my dad was indifferent about the fact that there were six knives stuck in the wall. He went to the kitchen and started rummaging through the cupboards for food. There was none. I marched alongside him. "Knives, Dad? Really? What on earth is wrong with you?"

"Skumpy, what's the big deal?" There was a slight slur in his words. I could tell the drinks were starting to hit home.

"What are you—in the circus? Are you crazy?"

He groaned, admitting to defeat by reason of no food in the house. "I'm going to bed."

I looked at the kitchen clock: half past three in the morning. It was just another late night/early day in the Garcia household.

4

Together

When Michael and I were a new couple, I remember a few instances when people made insinuating comments about his dealings with the Mob. I admit I was a little naive, so most times I didn't pick up on those clues, or whatever you want to call them. Hindsight truly is twenty-twenty.

One evening I was having dinner at Katie's parents' home, and my eyes were drawn to two items on their coffee table. One was a newspaper article about organized crime. There was nothing about Michael detailed in the article; it just talked about "the life."

During dinner, Katie's dad asked how Michael was. I didn't realize Katie had informed her parents of my dating status, but she later told me, "Yeah, I tell my parents everything." Then her dad made a telling remark along the lines of, "Aren't you scared of being his girl?" I thought maybe he was trying to warn me in the same way the dancers had, like I should be scared Michael would cheat on me or drop me like a hot potato. Looking back, I'm sure Katie's dad was referring to Michael's crime family connection, but at the time, his concern flew right over my head.

Our relationship moved rather quickly. I was talking to my mom almost every other day and told her the big news of us being an item. She asked me a lot of questions about Michael that I freely answered. One of the biggest strengths in our relationship was how my mom and I communicated. I trusted and appreciated her opinion, so I wanted her to know what was going on in my life. I didn't have to hide much from her that might have made her mad or disappointed in me.

During the last month or so of filming, Michael moved the cast and crew to another hotel. He also had the misguided idea to have all of my stuff moved into a room that adjoined his suite. The nerve! What was he thinking? I was outraged and told him so.

Michael tried to calm me down. "But I thought you'd be happy about it! And it's not like you don't have your own private room."

I was floored. "But there's no lock. You can come in and out of my room as you please, and I'm just not ready for that yet." Michael had a lot more to learn about me. Movie set or not, I was nowhere near ready to move in with him. "What will my mother say? Do you know how disappointed she'd be? Besides, we just started dating, Michael." He booked me another room that afternoon.

Filming was about to end, and I knew Michael and I had to talk about the future. What it held, I wasn't sure. I knew I wanted to be with him, but I had no idea the price I would have to pay for that. You never know what you can handle until you are forced to deal with whatever life happens to dish out.

But back in the spring of 1984, the biggest challenge I thought

Michael and I had was the fact that we lived on opposite coasts. Would one of us move? How would a long-distance relationship work? I knew Michael wanted to pursue a serious relationship, but I didn't know how the logistics of it all would play out. Soon enough, Michael would answer all these questions for me.

Knights of the City Jasmine's Bad Girls.
I'm the one on Michael's right.

Smokey, Me, and Michael, *Knights of the City* (1984).

5

Taking the Next Step

I loved taking drives with Michael. We were always going somewhere when he had a break from filming and I had a break from rehearsing. We'd speed down the picturesque highways in his convertible, with the wind blowing through my hair and the hot sun roasting the white leather seats. I'd snuggle up to him and relish in the fairy tale it seemed I was living.

On one of these rides, I told him he was going to marry me. It may have seemed like an audacious move, but what can I say? I just knew it. In the deepest part of my heart, I knew ours wasn't a superficial fling or a heat-of-the-moment affair that typically blossoms from movie sets. This was the real deal.

We stopped at a red light and were laughing, talking, and sharing funny stories about our family. A man stood a few feet away from Michael's car, carrying a large metal can of long-stemmed roses for sale. In his charming and friendly way, Michael motioned for the guy to come over. The flower guy barely spoke a lick of English, so Michael handed him a hundred-dollar bill and grabbed all the roses in the bucket. There were about forty of them, and they were all gorgeous, flaunting their vibrant ruby color and perfect bloom.

I couldn't stop smiling. "Michael, I can't believe you just bought me all those beautiful roses."

"They're not as beautiful as you, Cammy."

I nuzzled his neck and took a deep breath. Softly, I whispered, "Michael Franzese, someday you are going to marry me."

He intertwined his fingers with mine and squeezed my hand. "You know what? I think you're right, Camille. I think you're absolutely right."

I was in love with Michael for many reasons. He had the qualities I was looking for in a great man—kindness, warmth, generosity, respect. He was also hardworking—and romantic. And coming from my turbulent background, I valued the fact that he was a man of his word. Michael did what he said he would do. He showed up when he said he was going to show up. He kept his promises. I adored him with my whole heart, and there was no doubt in my mind that I wanted to spend the rest of my life with him.

My cousin Ted always encouraged me to find love in the right places, with a man who was motivated and doing something with his life. He'd tell me, "Cammy, you're a bright, intelligent, and beautiful girl. Hang out with the right people. Look for the right man. Make the right choices. Fall in love with someone who is going somewhere. Don't put yourself in a dead-end situation." After watching my father generate a string of bad choices that left his family suffering at times, I made a commitment to myself that I would never live that kind of life. I wanted a future that was promising, hopeful, and full of possibilities. And I knew Michael was a part of that future.

Every now and then, in this man who seemed to have the world in his palm, I noticed a faraway pain in his eyes. Like he was troubled somewhere in his spirit, a down-reaching place that he could not share with anyone, not even me. In a weird way, I was attracted to that sadness. I didn't know from where it originated and what dark places he was keeping from me, but I was sure I could bring light to those shadows.

When the filming of *Knights of the City* ended in the middle of 1984, Michael threw a huge wrap-up party. It was an elaborate affair at a unique venue, a Fort Lauderdale skating rink, with a guest list that included entrepreneurs, hot shots in the entertainment industry, and even celebrities. The local media gave the party a lot of well-deserved attention. We in the cast and crew basked in the limelight. After months of hard work, we felt we could all finally cut loose, relax, and revel in the fruits of our labor.

I spent most of the evening dancing and laughing with my dancer friends and bumping into random celebrities like Muhammad Ali and Emmanuel Lewis. Michael was constantly surrounded by a slew of serious-looking people in gorgeous Italian suits, but I didn't mind. I was having a blast with my girlfriends.

Toward the end of the evening, I noticed Michael was whisked away by a TV crew. It appeared they were interviewing him, but with the party still in full swing, it was difficult to get within earshot and find out exactly what the fuss was about. I didn't want to seem nosy, so I watched from a safe distance. What I saw alarmed me.

An austere reporter, who didn't crack a smile the whole time he was hammering away his questions, was clearly disturbing Michael. Always a man to control his emotions and remain cool, calm, and collected even in the most volatile of circumstances, Michael was getting fidgety and flustered. I didn't like the feel of what was happening. As preoccupied as Michael was, he noticed my unease and asked his good friend Louie to drive me home immediately. I was a little bummed because I didn't intend for this momentous evening to end with me leaving the party early (and by myself). I asked Louie if he knew anything about that interview, and he said something vague: that it probably had to do with Michael's father.

Sonny was a sore spot for Michael, and at that time he was desperately fighting to get his dad out of jail. Sonny is still in prison to this day. I tread carefully around the topic of Michael's relationship with his father because it is so sensitive. When he and I met in the morning, I didn't say a word about the fiasco, and Michael didn't either. Some things are better left unsaid.

Before filming officially came to a close, we talked about our future. Michael asked me question after question to better understand how I felt. "Where do you want to go from here?" "What are you going to do when you get home?" "What do you think about us?" I knew I wanted to continue our relationship—that much was obvious—but I also had plans I wanted to see through.

I wanted to go home to California, get my Firebird fixed, find a small apartment, and maybe even reenroll in school. Since being in Florida, I had acquired a refreshing sense of independence, and I wanted a chance to experience that self-sufficiency. It made me feel that I could do anything I put my mind to, especially pursue the dreams that had stirred my heart since I was a little girl.

When I aired my thoughts, Michael seemed impressed by my plans. He believed I could do all of those things . . . with him in the picture. "I want to meet your family," he told me. "Your dad seems incredibly interesting. Your mom sounds great. And your sisters and brothers seem like a blast to be around. What do you think if after a week or so of you being back in California, I flew out for a visit?"

I jumped up and hugged him. "Of course, Michael! My family is dying to meet you!" We are a big family and very close. My brother Dino and I are close in age and had fought like cats and dogs when we were young. Today we're the best of friends. Then there are Joaquin, Cuauhtemoc ("Temo" for short), and Che, all named by my father after revolutionaries and all of whom today serve the church. Joaquin is the pastor of a growing church, Dino is the executive pastor, and Che serves in the children's ministry. Five years younger than me is feisty Sabrina, who became my sidekick and still is, and last is Raquel, the baby of the family.

As kids we nicknamed ourselves the "Skeleton Crew" because of the many times we didn't have food in the house. Mitch, a close family friend, used to drop off pizza when he got off work at midnight. Whenever we knew he was going to stop by, we'd wait up for him until he showed up around one in the morning. Sure, we wouldn't get enough sleep to function at school the next day, but hey, we were going to eat. And the Skeleton Crew thought it was better to eat late than not eat at all.

When I left Florida and headed to Anaheim, I had some reservations about being home. Not that I didn't miss or love my family; I couldn't wait to see them. But there was a world of difference between living on a movie set in a luxurious hotel and living with your entire family in Small Town USA.

For starters, I had privacy. Prior to filming *Knights of the City*, I didn't understand the meaning of the word. I shared a three-bedroom, two-bathroom house with six siblings. Even a small task, like squeezing in more than a five-minute shower before a brother or sister (or two) was pounding on the door demanding I get out, was nearly impossible. In Florida, I had my own room. Not only that, but I also always had extra cash on me. And, of course, I was wined and dined by a fabulous man whom I fell in love with. Compared to Anaheim, Florida seemed like an unreal world that could only exist in my imagination.

My homecoming was heartwarming. It felt great to have all my brothers and sisters run into my arms and hug and kiss me. It was a special moment when I realized how much I had missed them. The reunion made me appreciate the closeness I shared with them. We may not have had much as far as material possessions growing up, but we always had each other. We were bonded for life, and even though sibling spats were frequent, they never lasted long. We were quick to lean on our loyalty as a family and never allowed stupid or petty arguments to cripple our kinship.

The first few days were like a little piece of heaven. I was excited to be able to give my family a portion of what I made filming the movie. I didn't do it out of obligation or because I felt forced; I helped my family because I knew it was the right thing to do, and I wanted to do it. I stocked our fridge with food, bought my siblings some clothes, and dined them in what they thought were fancy restaurants. By day three, however, the honeymoon was over. I felt cramped and couldn't wait to get my own apartment, go back to school, and start my own life.

After a week, Michael came to visit. I had missed him like crazy and couldn't wait to see his handsome face. Given my family's colorful background, however, I had some hesitation. I was also acquainted with his lavish lifestyle, so a part of me wondered how Michael would adjust to our humble way of life. We didn't have the kind of pomp and circumstance I know he was used to.

I warned Michael that when he showed up, he'd notice our house was the loudest and most crowded in the neighborhood. The Garcia home was a favorite hangout with the young kids around the block. And because our family loved to dance, there was always a dance-off going on in our driveway at any time of the day. Between the loud music blaring out of our garage and kids littering our lawn, experimenting with new break-dancing moves, our house was always bustling with chaotic energy.

Dino joined me when I met Michael at the Westwood Marquis. I practically knocked Michael down in my excitement. He wrapped his strong arms around me, and for the first time in a week, I felt safe, at ease, and protected. Whenever I hugged Michael, I felt the essence of home. He was my home. He was my rock. He was my shelter. And now he was in my neck of the woods, meeting who I hoped would be his future in-laws.

Later that evening, we drove to my parents' house. I was nervous because Michael is a lot older than I, and I wondered what my siblings would think of him. When Sabrina first met him, she did a double take. Then her gaze moved slowly from me to Michael and back to me. "He's kinda old," she blurted out. We couldn't help but laugh.

My siblings took to him immediately. Here was their big sister's boyfriend, a grown-up man who not only was good-looking, sharp, and well dressed; he was also super nice and funny. They loved him, and he returned the affection and treated them like his own brothers and sisters. They even showed him a few dance moves.

Michael and I took my parents out to dinner at the Black Angus, a popular steak joint in town. My mother, true to her character, was quiet most of the evening. She listened very intently while Michael, who did most of the talking, chatted with my dad. My dad had a lot of crazy stories to share about his days in the gangs and the near-death trouble he frequently found himself in. Needless to say, he kept Michael entertained. While we were enjoying our mouth-watering filet mignons, Michael had a heart-to-heart talk with my parents about his intentions to marry me. It made me feel even more secure in our future.

My parents had no idea of Michael's ties to organized crime. In fact, they knew about as much about this facet of crime as I did, which was pretty much nothing. Whatever insight we had into the Mob world came from movies like *The Godfather* or stories from our history books about infamous Mafia figures like Al Capone. You have to remember that while Mob dealings were pretty publicized in New York, we didn't hear about things like that in California. Where we lived, Hollywood, not gangsters, was the big enchilada.

If Michael would have told my dad the truth about his life and how he was going to get out of it, I doubt it would have made a difference either way. Fred would have loved him just the same. My dad was a revolutionary, a radical individualist who respected people because they were different and marched to the beat of their own drum. I think he would have even hailed Michael as an idol for trying to beat the system. I'm confident that if Michael's secrets had been brought to light, both of my parents would have nonetheless supported our marriage and our future together. My mother was a believer in second chances and forgiveness. She would say that the foot of the cross is level for everyone. And although she absolutely wouldn't have agreed with Michael's former lifestyle, knowing that there would be many consequences for it, she also believed that God's hand was in the midst of Michael's life.

My father liked Michael from the start. Between bites of juicy tenderloin, they spoke for hours about football, boxing, and the Yankees. I knew my dad well and had a feeling he was thinking, *Now, here is a man who can give my daughter a good life.* He could see Michael was a good guy. Frankly, there was nothing not to like about my future husband. Anyone who met him liked him. He had a way with people that was genuine and affable. My dad seemed convinced that Michael was my avenue to get the life he thought I deserved.

That night, Michael and I went back to his hotel in Westwood. My mom didn't want me staying there without a "chaperone," so I took my four-year-old sister, Raquel, along. Michael had to leave the next day for New York, but he told my sister and me to stay in the room as long as we wanted and to enjoy the lavish digs. We took advantage of the king-size bed, a bed so large that Raquel was positive she could live in the plush oasis for the rest of her life. We ordered room service and watched movies until the early hours of the morning. Raquel relished every moment and was so grateful for her big sister's "rich" boyfriend.

Michael eventually bought a condo in Brentwood, about forty-five minutes from Anaheim, which my other sister, Sabrina, and I moved into. The brand-new, two-bedroom condominium was ours to decorate. I had full reign of what colors would adorn the walls and what kind of furniture would represent my taste. I chose salmon for Sabrina's room and lavender (think mid '80s; trust me: lavender was a trendy color!) for mine. It was the opposite of what was written.

The interior designer presented me with a list of high-end stores that sold fabulous furniture. I went to one of them and was taken aback when I saw an exquisite but very uncomfortable-looking couch that was selling for four grand. I knew Michael wouldn't mind, but I could hear my mom's voice in the back of my head, warning me that it was a frivolous purchase (worse than choosing a $30 hamburger for lunch). I walked out of the store, crumpled up the list of expensive furniture boutiques, and marched straight down to a furniture chain store that sold reasonably priced pieces. I was happy with what I found.

When my friend Katie came to visit me from Florida and asked where I got my furniture, she couldn't believe it. "Cammy, your budgeting days are over. You don't have to shop at discount stores anymore!"

"What? You don't like how I decorated the place?"

"No, no. It's not that. You did a beautiful job! It's just that money is not an issue for you anymore. Get it through your head. If you find a five-thousand-dollar couch that you like, guess what? You can buy it!"

I knew what she was saying, but I certainly didn't want to spend Michael's money in unnecessary ways, even though he was very generous. And I could never justify spending seven thousand dollars on a dining room table or fifteen thousand on a bedroom set. It seemed irrational. Why would I spend an arm and a leg when only my sister and I lived at the condo? We certainly didn't care how opulent our apartment looked or what fancy, custom-designed chair sat in the corner of our living room.

While I was enjoying my new place, Michael was still flying back and forth to New York. Sometimes I was lucky to have him to myself for a few days, but there were many trips he would fly in with just enough time to take me out to dinner and head back to the airport to catch a red-eye back to New York. I wished it didn't have to be that way. I hated spending what felt like five minutes with him while he scuttled to his hometown to take care of things.

I did know there were still a lot of legal problems going on with his dad. And I knew he had children from his first marriage that he had to see. I always encouraged Michael to be involved in their lives, so I never wanted to seem selfish and complain that he wasn't spending enough time with me in California. All things considered, he was doing the best he could.

In the summer of 1984, Michael was arrested. The federal government slapped him with seven counts (I didn't find out the details of the indictments until years later) of loan-sharking and racketeering. I didn't know what it meant, so when I went to visit him in New York, he explained it to me. Truthfully, I didn't think much of it. Getting arrested and getting in trouble with the government were something I had seen on and off in my life with my father and my uncles. There was nothing disconcerting enough to make me even consider backing out of the relationship.

For the next few months, I traveled back and forth to New York from California. Sabrina kept me company most times. While

Michael waited for his trial date, which would end up taking almost four months to be scheduled, he continued to wine, dine, and profess his love to me.

In December of that year, he proposed. Some might argue we spun our relationship on the fast track, but we were in love. And we knew what we wanted—each other. I knew our engagement was coming because for a month or so he kept asking me questions about what kind of stones and cut I liked. Now, back then I couldn't tell you the difference between a princess or an oval cut or platinum or white gold. I didn't know a darn thing about the fine art of diamond shopping.

We'd walk into jewelry store after jewelry store and I'd stand paralyzed, blinded by the endless rows of bling that illuminated the black velvet and glass showcases. All the rings looked gorgeous, big, and shiny. Did I really have to figure out what I liked and didn't like? What was not to like about any diamond ring? I ended up telling Michael I was a fan of the emerald cut. I liked the way it looked on my hand.

One evening, he took me to Peppone, a romantic Italian restaurant in Brentwood, California. I was getting suspicious because the host and waiters were extremely attentive. They were all smiles as soon as we walked through the doors, and never stopped the entire evening. We frequently ate at that mouthwatering joint, so everyone who worked there knew us and were always friendly; but their warmth that day seemed particularly over-the-top. I was going to scream if I saw one more person come to our table and ask, "Can I get you anything else, Camille?" "Would you like a refill on your water?" "How about another glass of wine, Michael?" "More bread?"

As I bit into a delicious pasta dish that melted in my mouth with all its buttery and cheesy glory, Michael slid a black box right next to my bursting plate. I chewed my last bite fast but carefully (no girl wants to choke on fettuccine when she is proposed to by her beau).

My heart raced. I was nervous. Not because of the question that I knew was coming any second, but because of what was in the box. I didn't want to open it. I was afraid that I'd find a sparkler the size of half of my hand. I wanted something nice, of course, but I didn't want an obnoxious rock that could be seen from across a room.

Michael said, "If anyone had ever told me that someone like you, Camille, was going to come into my life and turn it upside down, and make me never want to leave L.A., I would have told them they were completely out of their minds. But that is exactly what you have done, and now I want to spend the rest of my life with you."

"I would love to marry you, Michael." And with that he put the lovely ring on my finger. (I eventually had to pawn the stunning 4-carat, emerald-cut diamond with baguettes on both sides for $75,000 the second time Michael went away. It took me eight years to get it back.) It was a magical moment I'll never forget. Classical music played in the background, and the waiters who celebrated the milestone with us finally left us alone so we could savor the special occasion with our favorite champagne, Taittinger Rosé. This was it. I had found my Prince Charming, and now we were officially on our way to forever.

While I tried not to let Michael's legal troubles interfere with my cloud-nine state, the truth was, I was worried about him being on trial. I knew that if we did get married and he got convicted, he would get more than a slap on the wrist; he could spend a long time in prison. But two people in my life made a huge effort to shift my worry into optimism—Michael and my mother.

Michael always made light of his state of affairs. It was his way of dealing with potential problems. Every time I questioned the trial, he immediately put my mind to rest. "Cammy, everything is going to be fine. Don't worry. Let's just enjoy each other." Early on in our relationship and even through Michael's first imprisonment,

I rested comfortably in his confidence. If he was sure about something, so was I. If he told me everything was going to be okay, I believed him. If we had been on a plane and the pilot voiced over the loudspeaker that the plane was going down, Michael could have somehow convinced me the plane was not going down.

In *Capture His Heart*, Proverbs 31 Ministries president and best-selling author Lysa TerKeurst talks about how even a great husband makes a poor God. "It is so important to get your every deep, spiritual need met by God alone. My husband can't give me this type of consistent love, joy, peace, etc. And I can't give him love, joy, peace, patience, . . . and self-control apart from Christ. Apart from Christ I can do no good thing, because apart from Christ I wither as I try to make my husband fill me. When I do this I drain my husband and my marriage."[1]

For the longest time, I put Michael above God. I allowed myself to place my confidence, my peace, and my assurance in a human being (even though he is a great man) instead of the One I had made the Lord over my life. This is a big mistake I see many women make. I want to tell you from painful experience that there is no one who can give you the peace, comfort, and love that can only come from Christ. Not a pastor, a best friend, or even a great husband. No man can ever fill your deepest needs or longings. Only God can. When we place so much expectation on a person to fill our empty spaces, we are only setting ourselves up for disappointment. This can make us question ourselves, the person we esteem above God, and even our faith.

I admit I was naive back then, but Michael had proven himself many times to me. His word was solid: he did what he said he would do. He'd moved the sun, moon, and stars for me. So after a

---

1 Lysa TerKeurst, *Capture His Heart: Becoming the Godly Wife Your Husband Desires* (Moody, 2002), 18.

few conversations with him calming my fears of being left alone, I finally stopped worrying about it.

My mother was equally confident that Michael would not get convicted. Her confidence did not lie in man, however. It rested in God. My mom always prayed for Michael, and she never let him or me forget it. She treated him like a son from day one.

Mom was always concerned for his well-being, and one time, when she noticed him unusually stressed and bothered by something, she pulled him aside and said, "Michael, I know you work very hard and have a lot going on. I want you to listen to what I'm going to tell you. Give all these problems to God. Trust in Him. You can't do it all yourself. I know Cammy thinks you're Superman, but I know you're not. You can't keep walking around with the world on your shoulders." I'm sure Michael didn't fully appreciate the spiritual overtones of my mom's wisdom, but he did appreciate her evidence of support and love. He knew she wanted the best for him, and he took that to heart.

Michael grew up in the Catholic Church. He was an altar boy, celebrated his first Holy Communion and confirmation, and eventually graduated from Holy Cross High School in Flushing, New York. Strangely, he was the only one in his family who attended church; his parents made him go and no one else. And he always believed in God but never knew he could have a personal relationship with Him. It took Michael many years before he could really have that relationship with the Lord. During our marriage, I know he wanted and needed it, but he felt unworthy of it. The surrendering part was just not going to happen, because back then Michael felt that God helps those who help themselves, and you don't fully rely on Jesus. After seven years of hardship and lots of prayer from me and my mom, he finally started relying on God's Word rather than on his will. I felt that God couldn't truly use Michael until He broke him, and that happened in an ugly cell in MDC Los Angeles.

During the trial, which was held in New York and began in January 1985, Sabrina and I went by the courthouse in hopes of having lunch with Michael. It was a cold winter day. I wrapped the silver mink coat Michael had bought me for Valentine's Day tight around my body to defend against the arctic air. Though my sister had spent many weeks with me on the East Coast, she was still unaccustomed to the battering chill. You can take a girl out of California, but you can't take California out of a girl.

We froze our way up the intimidating concrete steps of the courthouse and walked around the empty hallways, our high heel shoes click-clacking on the linoleum floors and echoing throughout the quiet floor. We made our way to the courtroom and quietly took a seat in the back. The courthouse was majestic and serious, revealing beauty in an old-style craftsmanship with dark, rustic hardwood floors and oak finishing on the benches and moldings.

I eyed the defendant's table and tried to find Michael. There were about twenty men sitting at the long, rectangular table. I couldn't tell who was a defendant and who was an attorney. Finally, Michael happened to turn around, and our eyes locked. His demeanor betrayed mixed feelings. On one hand, he seemed happy to see me; on the other hand, he looked uncertain. I smiled and hoped that he could feel my love and support.

Within five minutes of our arrival, my attention was fixed on the man on the witness stand. The attorney questioning him said, "Can you please point out Michael Franzese?" My heart sank. I didn't know what the line of questioning was before I walked in, and I wasn't sure I wanted to find out. The witness pointed his finger toward the defendant's table, but at another man, an acquaintance of Michael's whom I had met once.

"That's him. That's Michael Franzese."

The attorney nodded his head, then asked, "Are you sure the man you are pointing to is Michael Franzese?"

The witness squirmed in discomfort and nervously rubbed his hands together. He shook his head. "No, I'm, umm, I'm not sure. No, wait." He then pointed his finger at another man sitting two seats down from my fiancé. "Yeah, that's him. That's Michael Franzese."

I was confused. What was Michael doing on trial with a witness who appeared to be testifying against him but couldn't even point him out? *This is ridiculous.* I grabbed my sister's hand and gestured toward the heavy oak door. "Let's go," I whispered. We waited outside for the rest of the morning until Michael came out. It wouldn't be the last time I would step into a courtroom.

We scheduled our engagement party at the five-star Hotel Bel-Air in Los Angeles. We didn't have much time to plan it, but when you have a lot of money, it's amazing how quickly and beautifully things can come together. It was a great party, with about a hundred and fifty guests in attendance. I was disappointed because Michael didn't invite his immediate family. As a matter of fact, he was adamant about not having them there. The topic was not open for discussion, so I never said a word about it.

Looking back, I can understand his reservation. His divorce was only recently finalized, and here he was, getting engaged to another woman—and a younger one at that. Michael didn't want to cause his ex-wife or children any drama, so he kept the extravaganza under wraps. I didn't think of that when I got engaged, however. When you're young, it's easy to find yourself wrapped up inside your own world; you only see what you want to see. I was hopelessly in love, and at the time, my attention was solely fixed on Michael and me.

As lovely as the party was, I couldn't escape the gnawing feeling about the ongoing trial. I knew that closing statements were not too far away, and I wasn't confident about a positive outcome. My mom was staying with me in a condo in Long Island. She kept drilling into me the fact that God was going to work out something marvelous in Michael's favor and that His hand rested upon my fiancé and even this case. And she never stopped reminding me to pray.

On the last few days of the trial, Michael was more nervous than usual. He seemed quiet and withdrawn. He also kept hugging me every few minutes and telling me he loved me. One morning before he left for court, he held me tight for about ten minutes straight. I didn't know it at the time, but it was his last day of trial. In a matter of only a few hours, he'd find out if he would be free to go, acquitted of all charges, or found guilty and sentenced to spend many years behind bars.

Later that afternoon, the phone rang. It was Michael. "I'm done for the day, and I'm coming home." His voice sounded confident and bright, nothing like that morning. "Tell your mom we're going out for a nice dinner tonight." I knew something good happened, because usually on Fridays he wouldn't come home from trial until about seven in the evening.

When Michael burst through the door an hour later, there was a big smile on his face. "Did you get the verdict?" I anxiously wanted to know. "Did everything work out?"

"You bet it did!"

"Praise God!" My mom gave Michael a warm hug, and the somber mood was filled with welcome relief. *We're home free,* I thought. *He's not in trouble. He's not going to jail. Everything in the world is okay. We can finally start planning our wedding and our life together.*

We set our wedding day for July 27, 1985. In May my mother, Michael, and I took a weekend trip to Las Vegas. We needed a mini vacation from the exhausting trial and wedding planning. As we were walking down the crowded main strip, mesmerized by the flashing lights and elaborate architecture of the hotels, my mother made a surprising suggestion. "Why don't you two get married here? You're together all the time, and you're madly in love. Why not?"

I balked at the idea, but Michael's face immediately lit up like a Christmas tree. When he noticed my hesitancy, however, he took a step back and said, "Well, we don't have to get married today."

I let out a sigh of relief.

He continued, "But how about tomorrow?"

That's some compromise.

I finally agreed after some convincing by my mom that it would be a good thing. I didn't think I had an appropriate dress to wear, but my mom said, "Who cares? Wear any dress. You brought so many with you!"

Michael and I exchanged our vows in a cute chapel inside Circus Circus. We chose that chapel versus the hundreds of others in town because we were told by a handful of "wedding experts" that it was the prettiest and least tacky one around. There was truth to the hearsay. The chapel wasn't cheesy like the ones you see on TV. It was a regular chapel with modest but beautiful and tasteful white décor. And the place was relatively quiet. No rowdy throngs of foolish young people making the biggest decision of their lives because they'd had too much to drink that day.

The ceremony was short, simple, and sweet. I felt a twinge of regret for only one thing. One person, actually—my father. To this day, he still reminds me how I left him out of one of the most important days of my life. I didn't do it on purpose, of course. Sure, I wanted my dad there, but the wedding was impromptu. Mom kept telling me not to worry about my dad. "He'll understand," she assured me.

I was already pregnant with Miquelle when we took that trip to Vegas. Michael and I were ecstatic but kept our news a secret.

Later, when I told my mom, she swore she had a feeling during the trip that something was going on. And when we told my dad, he made sure to remind us how insulted he was about being left out of the wedding; then he congratulated us and announced with confidence, "I'm going to have a grandson. No doubt in my mind. We're having a boy."

Michael and I still wanted a big hoorah to celebrate the rest of our lives together, so we kept our official wedding as planned. More than four hundred people packed the elegant ballroom at the Beverly Hilton hotel that day. Sparkling crystal chandeliers showered down from the ceilings like diamond teardrops. Exotic flowers, flown in from Fiji that morning, colored the tables and spare corners of the ballroom.

Michael Jackson and Prince impersonators entertained and mingled with the crowd. For those with dancing fever (myself included), we provided a band for the older folks and a funky DJ for the young at heart. The buffet tables displayed three different types of cuisine: Italian, Mexican, and American. Whatever you fancied that night, it was sure to be on one of the stations. I had a blast, and while I was dying to spend most of the evening dancing, it's hard to ignore four hundred guests. Not that I even wanted to. The traditional Mexican dollar dance was hilarious. Friends and family each pinned a dollar bill on my five-thousand-dollar imported wedding dress to have a dance with me. By the time I accepted the last dance, you couldn't even tell what color my dress was; there were so many dollar bills piled on.

On our honeymoon in Hawaii, I made Michael promise to leave his beeper at home. Since the day we were introduced, his pager was constantly going off. There was no way we were going away for a week to paradise only to have me stuck listening to that *beep-beep-beep* go off at odd hours of the day. For one week, we finally had a chance to be alone and catch our breath. No mom. No dad. No brother or sisters. No trials. No legal problems. No late-night trips to New York or California. It was just Michael and me, alone in one of the most beautiful places in the world.

We enjoyed every moment. I'm glad we did because it wouldn't be long before I'd have to spend four years of my life without him. In only a few months, Hawaii would seem like a distant memory. Almost like a dream.

6

When Everything Started to Change

The few months after the honeymoon were a blur. At first, Michael and I were still traveling back and forth to opposite coasts. I was hoping things would settle down and we would have a more stable life. Even though we had an apartment in New York, we both loved Los Angeles, and things always seemed much easier when we were there, so I was hoping that we could go to California and actually stay put for a while. But things didn't pan out as I planned.

Sabrina, age fifteen then, was my companion on my frequent trips to New York. I spent a good chunk of time in Long Island and even enrolled her in school so she could get an education while visiting with me. Michael knew Sabrina was part of the package when he married me. He loved that my sister kept me company while he was working or out of town and always went out of his way to make her feel welcome. If Michael sent me flowers, he would send her a smaller version. If he sent me a box of chocolates, he'd send her some candy too.

I probably spent more time in New York than my hometown, but it had some advantages. I got to know Michael's family a little better. His sister Gia came over a lot and watched movies with me. Gia and I were very close. She was always the center of attention whenever she walked into any roomful of people, and she loved every minute of it. She confidently tossed her long, dark hair around her slender frame and exuded a natural sexiness. She didn't have to try very hard for people to notice her exotic Italian beauty. It came easy for her. Sadly, Gia died of a drug overdose when she was in her midtwenties. I still miss her so much.

I was also close to Michael's siblings John and Tina, more so than to his other brothers and sisters. John shared with me stories about what it was like growing up in the Franzese household. Through these eye-opening talks, I learned a lot about the dynamics of Michael's family, especially the difficult relationship he had with his parents.

Though he was followed by some dark shadows in his life, I thought John was a good guy. He was also a jokester at heart. He always had something funny to say that could lighten any mood, and I appreciated his humor. It makes me sad to think of how his relationship with Michael and his father slowly crumbled over the years. The youngest girl in Michael's family, Tina, died of lung cancer when she was only forty. I remember her as a sweet woman, very kindhearted and good-natured.

Michael spent more time in California when our first child was born. Miquelle came into our lives with a reckoning force on November 25, 1985. It was a difficult birth. I was in labor for a good twenty-four hours and was grateful to have Michael by my side. He was a great calming force (as much as you can calm a woman giving birth), and we were proud to welcome our healthy baby girl into our family.

I know all mothers are biased, but my daughter was a beautiful baby. I could never walk her down the street without someone stopping us every ten minutes and begging for a peek at her chubby little happy self. Miquelle was a bundle of joy from her thick head of dark hair to her plump legs.

While I was adjusting to the life-changing facets of being a first-time mother, another major change was on its way. The old saying is true that there is only one constant in life, and that is change. I didn't know it at the time, but when our daughter was born, there was a ten-year ongoing investigation under way. Michael had beat the government at their own game four times before, and now federal officials were dead-set on putting him away in prison for life. They were committed to pinning some crime on him that would stick and guarantee a lengthy prison term. While the law was on Michael's tail when he was or wasn't looking, I was too busy enjoying newlywed life. But not for long.

Michael left the house early on the morning of December 16, 1985. I didn't know the reason for his sudden departure, but I didn't think much about it. I just rolled over and went back to sleep. What I didn't know was that the feds were after him. A bunch of Michael's associates had already been arrested, and his name was next on the list. It was only a matter of time before he was arrested.

Later that day, I got a phone call from Michael. What he would tell me would change my life forever. "There is a federal indictment coming down the line. They're looking for me, Cammy; that's why I had to leave the house this morning. They'll be coming for me. I'm sorry." He told me of his plan to turn himself in and make bail in Florida.

As he was talking, I was trying to process what he was saying. It was an impossible task. *Wasn't he just acquitted? Why would he even need to turn himself in if he's innocent? If he turns himself in, does that mean he's going to prison? Is he leaving us?* I immediately recalled a conversation Michael and I had after his acquittal. In hindsight, I can see that it was a warning, but at the time his statement went over my head. He told me that the feds, specifically the Organized Crime Strike Force from the eastern district of New York, were more determined than ever to get him. They wanted to clobber him with the same racketeering, tax evasion, and loan-sharking charges that Rudy Giuliani had tried to pin against him.

The conversation reminded me of the many times my father would complain about the local cops. "They hate me," he'd always say. "They have it in for me. They're trying to get me any way they can." I thought of Michael's situation as similar to my dad's, but on a grander scale. I tucked away his caution in the back of my mind. Don't get me wrong; I was worried. But I was trying to live out my mother's teaching to stay positive and deal with the moment at hand, not worry about what could happen.

Not long after our conversation, I heard a knock at the door. We didn't get many visitors besides family members, and we always knew when they were coming. Sabrina curiously peeked through the peephole to see who was at the door.

"There's a bunch of men in suits," she whispered. "And they look serious."

This can't be good, I thought as I opened the door.

Four FBI agents stood in front of me. Their somber faces betrayed no emotion.

One of them flashed a shiny badge in my face. "Is Michael Franzese here?"

"No." I kept my answers curt.

"We're looking for him. Do you know where he is?"

"No, I'm sorry, but I don't."

The spokesman of the group strained his neck to get a glimpse of the inside of the condo. "Can we take a look around?"

I didn't see why not. I had nothing to hide. "Sure."

The FBI quartet walked into the hallway and took a couple of steps around, glancing in every direction but not conducting a thorough search. I didn't show it, but I was nervous. *This must be it. They've come to take him away.*

Within five or ten minutes of the loud knock, the men thanked me and left. Meanwhile, my sister—fascinated somewhat by the drama of FBI agents swarming around our condo—took watch by the window to see what these men in fancy suits were doing. She gave me a blow-by-blow playback of what was going on outside.

"One is pacing around the front door . . . Another guy is on the phone by his car . . . Oh, wait—and two of them are walking around the parking lot by the garages." I allowed my sister to revel in the action because I knew she didn't know the potential seriousness of the questioning. I'd rather her have a little fun than be alarmed about the whole thing.

I sat on the couch, trying to put together a plan. I couldn't just say good-bye to my husband over the telephone. I had to meet him. I was trying to figure out how I was going to discreetly leave the condo and head over to the Hotel Bel-Air (I knew he'd be there because he said he was staying at his favorite hotel), when I noticed that it had been quiet for a few minutes. Sabrina was nowhere to be found.

I rushed out the front door and saw her standing by the side of the condo, carrying a heavy bag of garbage and talking to one of the agents. No, wait—the two of them were flirting. He was leaning in her direction, smiling and acting overly friendly, very unlike the monotone, unemotional robot he acted like a few minutes earlier.

What is Sabrina doing? And what is this guy doing trying to move in on a minor? I was livid. This was unacceptable. There was no way these arrogant, bullheaded suits were going to come to our home uninvited, invade our privacy, and then have the audacity to flirt with my baby sister!

I angrily walked to Sabrina's side, and the agent, seeing the annoyed expression on my face, took a few steps back. I grabbed my sister's arm, almost knocking the trash to the floor with the force. "Sabrina!" I hissed. "Get back inside. Don't say another word." And without giving her the chance to say good-bye to the handsome young man, I marched her back into the condo, garbage bag in tow. I was so irritated I didn't even throw the smelly bag in the dumpster.

I had the feeling that if I left, the agents would immediately follow my trail. They weren't stupid. They knew I'd be itching to find my husband, so I'm sure they had me on close watch. Still, I wanted to confirm my suspicions. I walked out the front door and nonchalantly drove off to the grocery store. Sure enough, a glance in my rearview mirror gave me the evidence I needed that agents were on my tail. Their dark cars with tinted windows were not so inconspicuous. I bought some household products I didn't need, headed back to my car, and drove home. Their cars flashed like a neon sign in my rearview mirror. It was clear; I'd be going nowhere without their unwelcomed escort.

I figured I had no choice but to sneak out. I enlisted my sister as my eyes and ears. Sabrina planted herself stealthily behind the living room curtain and waited until all four agents were in plain view. When I heard her say, "Okay, they're all in front of the condo," I bolted. I ran to the back bedroom and crawled off the second-floor balcony. Holding on to the railing for dear life, I slid down as far as I could to the ground. I didn't want to jump any more than I needed to. Fortunately, I was athletic, or I'd never have been able to catapult myself out of the condo like that.

As far as I knew, no one saw me hop in my car and leave the complex. I went out to the back gate, through the alley, where only service vehicles were allowed to enter and exit, and sped down the highway to the hotel. I had packed some clothes for Michael in a small suitcase because I knew he would be on his way to Florida.

He was surprised and relieved to see me. We only had a few short hours together before I had to drive him to the airport for his flight to Fort Lauderdale. We ended up booking his ticket in my brother Che's name to avert the authorities that were scouting airline records for any outgoing flights under Michael's real name.

I cried the whole time, and Michael tried his best to console me. "What's going to happen to us? Who is going to take care of me and Miquelle? What are we going to do?" I was distraught, and my nerves were shot to a million pieces. Sitting on the hotel bed with my head in his lap, I was a wreck. I wasn't prepared. I wasn't ready. I didn't even know how to prepare myself for such a thing. How do you create a contingency plan for your family when your husband mentions out of the blue that he is going to jail? Where do you even start?

Michael cradled me and rubbed my shoulders, softly whispering, "It's going to be fine, Cammy. Everything is going to be okay. You'll see."

Through my sobs, I told him how upset I was because he couldn't see Miquelle one last time. "Oh, Cammy, she's too young to remember anything. Besides, she's safe at home with Sabrina. Don't cry. I promise I'll see you all soon." *Soon*, I repeated, trying desperately to comfort myself. *Me and Miq will see him soon.* And technically, he was right. But my understanding of "I'll see you soon" was for him to come home for good and us to be able to live out our dream lives. I would have never imagined "I'll see you soon" meant visiting him every weekend behind a glass pane or in a maximum-security prison in the middle of nowhere.

We barely spoke on the way to the airport. There was nothing to say. We held hands, and I clung to his so tight I think my nails left marks on his palm. When I had dropped him off at airports in times past, Michael would stand on the curb until I drove off, blowing kisses and waving at me until my car was a tiny dot on the horizon. This time was different. I drove off, my eyes glued to the rearview mirror, but all I saw was his back. He walked into the terminal without once looking back.

The tears continued to rain down my face as I drove home. But at some point the stronger, more sensible part of my nature took control. *Pull yourself together. You don't want Sabrina seeing you like this. It'll make her worried, and you being hysterical will only make Miq nervous.* At this point, I was so discombobulated that I didn't think of possible repercussions. My only concern was to help my husband. Luckily, the authorities didn't even notice me coming back in through the service area. They didn't want me; they wanted Michael.

Once I put my daughter to bed, and Sabrina was in her bedroom, getting her nightly fix of television, I called my parents and told them what happened. I could tell my mother was saddened and disappointed by the news. I don't think she ever anticipated Michael being arrested again.

They showed up at the house an hour or two later. My mom, the matriarchal pillar, enveloped me in her arms and repeatedly kissed my forehead like she used to do when I was a little girl. "Cammy, we're going to get through this. You have to be strong. We'll take this one day at a time and figure out what is going on. Pray and trust God, and be strong. He has this whole situation in His hands."

Mom was a fortress of spiritual strength. I was ready to jump out the balcony—and this time not in a gallant effort to rescue my husband—but my mom was a calming equilibrium and was able to work her magic on me to settle my emotions. She released me from the bear hug and gave me her signature gentle smile. In my heart, I knew everything would be okay, but for the life of me, I wasn't sure how. I had more questions than answers, but she was right. I'd have to trust God and let my questions sit for a little while. Obsessing over the whats and whys would do my daughter and me no good.

Eventually, Michael got sent to New York and was able to call me. He sat in jail at the Metropolitan Correction Center (MCC) and asked me to come see him. "Have your mom or Sabrina come with you. And pack enough stuff for a month. It'll take some time before we figure out what's going on."

Sabrina, the baby, and I flew into New York and checked into the hotel that Michael had arranged for us through his attorney, John Jacobs. The hotel, as luxurious as it was, was stodgy and depressing. Adorned with dark mahogany paneling, rich burgundy carpets, and heavy velvet curtains, it reminded me of the décor of old English royalty. There was nothing bright or whimsical about the place. I'm sure I would appreciate it more now, but back then it reminded me of the already dismal ordeal I was in. We spent one night there, and then through Michael's connections, we moved to Le Parker Meridien hotel off of Central Park. It was perfect.

The next day, I went to see Michael at the MCC. I left my little girl with Sabrina, as I didn't know what to expect. I had never visited anyone in jail before and felt like a fish out of water. Riding in the car service, I suddenly felt alone. Though I had visited New York hundreds of time, I was either with Michael, my mom, or one of my siblings. This time I was by myself. It was a weird feeling and one I didn't like very much.

The car slowed down in front of a faded brick building, nondescript except for the bold-lettered words *Metropolitan Correction Center* front and center over the entrance. The prison is located in downtown Manhattan on Park Row, behind the Thurgood Marshall U.S. Courthouse at Foley Square. It was home to a few famous inmates, including John Gotti, Bernie Madoff, and Ramzi Yousef.

I noticed a long line snaking along the sidewalk from the front door. *Strange.* I wondered what the line was for. *Maybe there's someone famous in there.* The driver let me out of the car, and I told him not to leave. "Wait for me," I asked him. "Please don't leave. Keep the car here."

"Of course, Mrs. Franzese," he reassured me. "Don't worry. I won't leave you." (I was starting to get annoyed hearing "Don't worry" all the time, but this time I needed to hear it more than ever.)

I took my place at the end of the line and shivered in my fur coat. It reminded me of visiting Michael at the courthouse when he was on trial almost a year earlier. Ahead of me stood thirty or forty mostly women and small children. They all looked irritated. I couldn't blame them. Who wants to stand in line in the freezing cold, only to get inside a dank, depressing prison? I certainly didn't.

My mind raced the entire two hours I stood in my high-heeled boots. *Am I really here? I can't believe I'm standing in line to see my husband in jail. Oh my gosh, my husband is in jail! Is this really happening?* I felt like the star of a Lifetime movie of the week.

Once inside, I went through a metal detector, filled out paperwork, waited some more, and finally, I was told to wait in the room where the prisoners would make their grand appearance. It was now three hours later. My ears rang with the noise of barked orders from sullen guards, the clanging of iron bars, the jingling of keys that hung from the guards' belts, and the whispers of visitors. But I was soothed by my favorite sound of all—the sweet chorus of children's chatter and laughter. I couldn't believe how many little kids were here to see their fathers (or some male figure in their lives). It was a bittersweet sound and made me miss Miq.

The visiting room was fairly large and minimally furnished. Only a few nailed-in tables and benches, where prisoners were already meeting with their visitors, dotted the floor, and a row of metal folding chairs, where the rest of us waited, lined the walls. Guards were secured in every corner and brandished nightsticks, guns, and I'm sure other weapons hidden in places none of us could see.

All the seats were taken, so I propped myself against a wall and waited. A big Italian guy came by and offered me a seat next to his mother. I politely declined, but he was persistent. "Please, miss. Sit by my mom. It's no trouble at all. Trust me: this whole thing is gonna take a while." How could I say no? I graciously accepted his kind offer.

This man's mother was a sweetheart. She took me under her wing for the ten minutes we had before Michael came in. "You're new here, right?"

I nodded and forced a nervous laugh. "It's that obvious, I guess?"

She moved closer to me and whispered, "Let me give you some advice, honey. The next time you come back here, and I'm pretty sure you'll be back, don't wear your beautiful jacket or jewelry. Leave your fancy stuff at home. Take it from me. You don't want to stand out. The less attention you draw to yourself, the better."

I looked down at my outfit and started to feel a little foolish. All of a sudden, my wedding ring and diamond necklace seemed to light up the drab room like the Macy's firework display. I self-consciously smiled and thanked her. Lord knows, the woman was right. Finally I heard my name over the loudspeaker.

And then I saw my husband from across the room. Sporting a jumpsuit that matched the beige of the prison walls, he wore handcuffs and was escorted by a tall guard who looked like he hated his job. The sight of Michael broke my heart. He looked helpless. All my selfish emotions were suddenly replaced by compassion. I felt terrible for him, and my eyes welled up with tears, especially because his hands were chained together and there was nothing he could do about it. He couldn't talk his way out of handcuffs. He couldn't call a friend to get him out of them. He couldn't do someone a favor to get free either.

The guard sat Michael down at one of the long metal tables and ordered me to sit opposite him. "No touching," he snapped. "And you've got thirty minutes."

Michael and I stared at each other for a few seconds, grateful to be able to sit in each other's company after so many days apart, even if it had to be under less-than-desirable circumstances. I broke the silence first and let out a machine-gun succession of questions.

"What's going on? How long do you have to stay here? When can you come back to Califor—?"

Michael interrupted my rambling. "Cammy, I don't want to waste time talking about this. John Jacobs is figuring it out for us. He'll be in touch. Look, we don't have a lot of time. Let's talk about other stuff. How are you? How's the baby?" He looked deep into my eyes and sighed. "Gosh I miss you."

Our allotted half hour passed by in a minute. Before I knew it, another guard swooped down on our table and told us, "Time's up, folks. You know the deal." And just like that, Michael was gone. I couldn't even hug or kiss him good-bye, but as the "gestapo" whisked him off, unlike at the airport, this time he turned around and smiled. That small gesture had enough power to melt my heart. I missed him already.

When I left the MCC, the rain fell in sheets, drowning the busy sidewalks and crowded streets. Mother Nature pounded out her violent fury on the city, drenching commuters on their way home from work and making rush-hour traffic even more unbearable than usual. All I could think about was holding Miq. I couldn't wait to see my precious baby. She was my saving grace, my comfort, my source of strength. When I nestled her sweet-smelling body in my arms, all of my troubles faded into a barely visible mist. Miq was my reminder that I needed to be strong and follow my mother's advice to take things one step at a time. Even if it meant one hour at a time or even one minute at a time.

I walked out of the elevator toward my hotel room and was startled by a bloodcurdling scream that ripped through the floor. It was my lovely daughter. An exasperated Sabrina shoved my wailing baby into my arms and said, "I can't take this anymore! She won't take a bottle. I tried everything, but she just won't eat, and she won't stop crying." My sister pointed to a row of every imaginable shape and size of bottle nipples on the table. "See, I even ran out and bought all this stuff, but nothing worked."

Poor Sabrina. And poor Miq. I was nursing at the time, and the fact that I had been gone for five hours completely escaped my mind. My sweet girl was starving, and only her mama's food would satisfy her hunger.

I called my mother later that night. I couldn't help but break down. "Why are you crying?" she asked. It wasn't that she didn't know the answer. She was making a good point. "Cammy, listen to me. I understand you are going through a rough time. It's tough. It's difficult. I get it. But you have to look at the brighter side of this picture. You are healthy. You have a beautiful and healthy daughter. And you have a family who loves and supports you."

I swallowed back the tears and tried to switch gears. I wanted to transform from focusing on the negative to reminding myself of the positive. It was a task I would force myself to repeat many times over.

"You have to be positive, Cammy," my mother continued. "Pick yourself up. Instead of thinking about what might happen, think about how wonderful it will be when Michael finally comes home. Think about what a kind and good-hearted man he is. Think about the good times you've shared and the good times you're going to share."

Mom paused and took a deep breath. "I'm not making light of what you're going through, but you have to remember that everybody goes through something. We all have trials, especially in marriage. Some people are hit with them five or ten years into the marriage; you happen to be hit with one a lot sooner. This is your lot, Cammy. This is what you chose for yourself."

Choices. It was always about choices. I made the choice to date Michael. I made the further choice to marry him and to spend a lifetime with him, for better or for worse. True, our "worse" was happening at the starting line of our marriage, but what could I really do about it? All I needed to focus on was being the best mom and wife I could be, no matter how bad things got. I couldn't crawl into a fetal position and hide in a closet until this mess went away.

I stayed in New York through January until we were able to get a handle on Michael's case. His hearing got postponed for weeks, so as he sat in jail, we were both kept in the dark about the pending investigation. During that time, Sabrina went back to California, and my mom took her place with me. We didn't do much during this time. My mom was content staying in the hotel room all day, playing with the baby, reading, and watching TV. I'd visit Michael at MCC about three times a week. I never took Miq with me because the standing in line and waiting around in the cold would have likely compromised her immune system and made her crabby.

My mom was annoyed that the hotel we were staying in was so expensive, and she wasn't shy about voicing her opinion either. She acted exactly how I did when I first started dating Michael and was flabbergasted at how much a small appetizer plate cost. It took some time for Mom to get used to room service. It was too fancy and too pricey for her taste, so we lived on Ray's Pizza during much of that time.

Despite my constant reminders that money wasn't an issue and that Michael had no problem paying whatever it cost for us to stay in New York, she'd vehemently protest, "No. I don't want Michael to pay for all this. It's ridiculous. We don't need all this stuff." I happened to look at the hotel bill when we checked out, and it was shocking. It ended up costing tens of thousands of dollars. I never said a word to my mom.

When Michael's arraignment was scheduled, he began to mull over a possible plea, against the persuasions of his attorney. I didn't know this at the time, but Michael wanted to take the plea as part of his plan to walk away from "the life" and live a new one with me in California. He also didn't want to take the chance of getting convicted and going to prison forever, which could have very well been the case. At least with a plea, he guaranteed our family some kind of future.

On one of our visits, Michael walked me through the nuts and bolts of a plea arrangement. "I'm trying to talk them [the government] into giving me some slack if I plead guilty. If I go to trial and lose, I could lose you and Miquelle for a long time. That's what happened to the other guys who got indicted for the same charges. I don't want what happened to them to happen to me. I've got too much at stake, Cammy. If I plea-bargain with the prosecutor, I could get ten years in prison, but at least I won't have to serve the entire sentence. I'd be away for only five years."

Five years. Five years. I thought it over. Five years was doable. Yeah, I could do five years versus ten, twenty, or even a lifetime.

"I might even be able to serve my sentence at Terminal Island, which is close to Los Angeles. I could be serving my sentence where we live."

Again, not a bad deal. I was distraught over my husband spending any amount of time in prison, but if I had to choose between the unknown (and quite possibly forever) or a prison term of a few years, I'd gladly choose the latter. Especially in light of the other defendants who had been found guilty and were serving a hundred years to life.

I knew what my gut was telling me, but I talked to my mom about it when I got back to the hotel. Her answer was typical. "Pray about it, Cammy, and see what God is leading you to do."

I groaned. I appreciated her spiritual insight, but pray about *this*? Really? Did God really care what choice I made? Did He really care how long Michael was in prison? Was there really a better way to get through this crisis depending on what decision I made? I doubted it.

"Mom, I gotta tell you. I don't think it's God's job to lead us in this decision. I think He's got more important things to worry about. I think it's our choice. Sure, He'll help us go through it, but I don't think He'll tell us what to choose, one way or another."

As much as I loved my mom and knew she was right most of the time, there were times, more so at the genesis of this ordeal, when I wanted her to tell me something other than "Pray about it." But here's the thing. There are so many situations in life we can't control and we can't change. And there is only one person who can control or change circumstances—God. So without prayer, where would we be? Probably floundering around, trying to sift through pains and problems with our own understanding and compass system. And most times, our navigation tools aren't so accurate.

"Stop worrying," my mom continued, "and start praying. If you worry yourself, you're going to get sick. And if you're sick, you won't be able to visit your husband, and you won't be able to take care of Miquelle. Whatever Michael is going through is out of your hands." She repeated her point with firmness. "Cammy, pray that God will lead you to make the right decision. Don't stop praying."

I believed what she was saying for the most part, but there was a small part of my core that revolted. *Where is God in this*? I shouted on the inside. *Is He even here? Is He intervening in some way?*

Whenever I uttered these questions out loud, my mom would ask, "Why are you blaming God? Why are you questioning Him?"

I felt even more frustrated. Why couldn't I be honest with God? Didn't He know exactly what I was feeling or thinking anyway? "But I can question, Mom, can't I? Isn't God big enough to handle my questions?"

"Sure, you can ask Him questions, Cammy. But remember, they're coming from a very angry place right now. Don't let your questions keep you from trusting Him."

"Well, of course I'm angry! Can you blame me?" Thankfully, our talks never ended with my pouting. Mom would always, and with such amazing grace, pilot our conversation back to choices, consequences, and prayer. We make choices, we have to deal with the consequences, so we always have to pray.

Though Michael was an altar boy and had attended Catholic school, his family wasn't practicing their faith. He did believe in God, but that was pretty much the extent of his spiritual background. I shared my faith with him, but I never force-fed it down his throat. Neither did my mother. We both felt the biggest testimony anyone can give is to be a living example of Christ. The life of faith is not marked by what we tell people we believe, but by how we live.

From the day my mother met Michael, she truly believed there was a purpose and reason why he was in our lives. When we first starting dating, she would tell me, "Cammy, I don't know much about Michael, where he came from, or what his family is like, but I know that someday he is going to be a man of God. One day Michael Franzese is going to travel all over the country and share his testimony with millions of people. And he is going to tell them how God changed his life." I thought she was nuts, but she never wavered in her faith.

During the years Michael spent behind bars, she frequently reminded me of this mysterious (and, at the time, dormant) call that God had on Michael's life. She never doubted, not even for a second, that God was going to work out the situation for His glory. She didn't question it even when we were hit by unexpected setbacks and were faced with the possibility of Michael spending more time in prison than we anticipated.

Whatever the obstacle or mountain that stood before us, Mom would confidently believe that God had closed a door because a better opportunity was right around the corner. She showed me compassion and prayed me through my moments of sadness and anger. If it hadn't been for her and her unquenchable passion and belief in prayer, I would have never been able to get through the next ten years.

Before my mom died, she was able to witness the fruits her prayers had birthed. She saw Michael give his testimony in churches a couple of times. Though she didn't get to see the extent of my husband's ministry—which keeps on growing and never fails to amaze me—God gave her a glimpse of the gift of her faithfulness and humbled me by the truth that things—great things, powerful things, and things we cannot do on our own—can happen when we stand firm in prayer.

Michael ended up signing a ten-year plea but thankfully would only have to serve five. He was allowed to fly back to Los Angeles and spend three months at a halfway house before he was officially sentenced. (I don't think they offer these arrangements anymore.) Michael stayed at that house during the night and spent the rest of the day with our family.

But we were never alone. The government didn't want to take any chances and had us followed by U.S. marshals everywhere we went. Whether it was to the beach, the mall, my parents' house, or even Miquelle's christening, officers shadowed our every move. It didn't bother me a bit. I could have had an army following me; I was just happy that I got to spend time with my husband before he left. I knew the three months would pass by in a blink of an eye, and it wouldn't be long before Michael would be gone.

We did get to celebrate a new addition before he went away. I was pregnant again. I can't tell you my immediate reaction was joy. I was frustrated because of the horrible timing. After all, my husband was going away to prison. Michael, thankfully, did not share my sentiment. He was excited and thought it was the perfect time to move out of Brentwood and, at least while he had a few weeks left, pave the way for a new life in a new place.

Luxury, high-rise condominiums were beginning to be built on the Wilshire Corridor, famously known as the "Golden Mile." One of the most desirable high-rise streets in the world, it stretches from west of the Westwood Village to the east of the boulevard of the Los Angeles Country Club. The panoramic views of the Pacific Ocean were impossible to describe and left me speechless at the wonder of God's beautiful creation. It was high-rise living at its finest. The biggest selling point for Michael was the twenty-four-hour security offered at the Mirabella, the building we liked most. We closed in a matter of days. It was official. We were finally getting a home of our own.

The builder had a slew of business cards of interior designers he highly recommended. "Who's your best one?" Michael asked.

"Sherry Shlesinger," the builder replied. "But honestly, she's in such high demand, I doubt you'll get her."

Not one to be discouraged, Michael told him, "Give me Sherry's card. I only want the best."

I don't know what Michael said when he called her, but Sherry agreed to design our home and got started on the demanding project right away. I have a feeling it had something to do with money. As naive as I might have been, I knew money could talk.

As we were preparing our new digs, NBC broke a story about Michael that abruptly aborted his comfortable situation in California. He was shipped back to New York one afternoon after receiving a call to report to the U.S. Marshal's office.

He wouldn't return for another forty-eight months.

July 1985

My siblings, "The Skeleton Crew"

7

Finding Out the Truth

While I was trying to envision a new life of parenting two kids with a husband in prison, Michael had other things on his mind. He was quitting the Mob, as the NBC story had said. I didn't know about his decision because I didn't know the extent of his involvement with the organization. Frankly, I didn't know he was even involved.

Yes, I was naive. Maybe I subconsciously turned a blind eye to the warning signs that may have been present. Maybe I didn't want to believe that Michael could be the man the government was painting him to be. Whatever the case, I believed my husband was under the federal radar for white-collar crimes. He didn't kill anybody. He didn't kidnap anybody. He didn't commit any sort of violent act against an innocent person. My thinking was, he simply cheated the government out of some money. I'm not saying it was right or justifiable, but that's why he was in trouble.

During that time, Michael found himself at the onset of a long-winded battle. A battle in which he'd have to wrestle with demons—from his past, from his former connections, from his current associates, and from his bad decisions. Michael kept our relationship separate from the war he was waging in order to protect our family. I'm sure he didn't want me to have to think about anything Mob-oriented; all he wanted me to focus on was raising our children in the midst of a legal circus.

I get asked all the time, "You really didn't know he was in the Mob?" I didn't. Really. Don't get me wrong. I had some suspicions. When I was staying in New York during part of our engagement, I saw a couple of newspaper headlines about organized crime. A few of them had to do with friends of Michael whom I'd met once or twice getting killed. One of them got gunned down in cold blood in front of his own home. When I read this, shivers crawled up and down my spine. My imagination ran wild. The biggest question that haunted me was, *Will someone do this to Michael?*

I had to ask him about it. I held the paper in front of his face and asked, "Michael, do you know something about this? This guy got shot right in front of his house. Are you in any way connected with what happened?"

His eyes darkened a bit, and there was a heaviness in his voice. "No." I could tell the incident was pulling on a heartstring or two even though he tried to act nonchalant. He never gave me any more details, so I dropped the subject. Michael was similarly terse in his answers to my questions concerning his work and even his court case. It encouraged me to keep my mouth shut and not pry or dig deeper.

And then there were the rumors. A few people from the set of *Knights of the City* and random people I knew through the years whispered about Michael's connections with organized crime. They always used that particular term or "crime family." I never heard the words *Mob* or *Mafia* actually spoken or written. Frankly, I didn't have a clue what "organized crime" was. It didn't make any sense to me. Of course crime was organized. How could crime be disorganized? I figured anyone with half a brain could organize crime.

Years later I started to understand what "Mafia" meant and the kind of life it involved when Michael was writing his first book, *Quitting the Mob*, which was released in 1993. His ghostwriter was living in our guesthouse for six months and working with Michael on his story. One morning I went to tidy up the writer's living space and make sure he had enough fresh towels and that his refrigerator was stocked with plenty of water and food. As I walked into his office, I literally stepped on handwritten notes he had strewn all over the floor. I picked up one sheet of paper and read something about Sonny Franzese being a crime boss, that he had been convicted of conspiracy to commit bank robbery, and that he had also been accused and tried (but found not guilty) of murder.

I felt a lump in my throat and thought I was going to be sick. But curiosity got the best of me, and I picked up another yellow sheet of paper and read something about Michael being in the Colombo crime family. My heart pounded. I quickly tossed the note back where it came from. I wanted to be as far away from that piece of paper as I possibly could. I wanted to pretend I never even picked it up.

It was the first time I officially saw my husband's name associated with the Mob and with a specific family. It was then I finally realized there was a lot more to Michael than I had known up to this point. I was overwhelmed by this revelation and just shut down. I didn't want to know anything else. I didn't want to know the details. I didn't want to know the whole truth.

A few years ago, when I read Michael's book *The Good, the Bad and the Forgiven* in what I believe was a God-ordained accident, I finally came to grips with the fact that I couldn't escape the reality of his involvement with the Mob. I was at a church where Michael was scheduled to speak. He is constantly on the road, traveling and speaking. I usually go with him to help with scheduling or merchandise sales, so I always pack a book or two to keep me occupied. This time, however, I came empty-handed.

As Michael spoke, I sat at the merchandise table and, not having anything to do until the service ended, I picked up the tiny book. Besides being bored out of my mind and frustrated because I hadn't packed at the very least a magazine, I don't know what possessed me to read the book. I had never read anything Michael has written, not *Blood Covenant* or even any newspaper or magazine articles about him.

I was blown away by what I read. It was like a crash course in the life of organized crime. There I was, sitting in a church foyer, getting schooled on Mafia 101, while my ex-mobster husband was preaching about his spiritual transformation. Yes, I'd been married to him for twenty-five years, and yes, I'd heard him give his testimony many times. But when I read this book, I entered into a dark world I never knew existed—Michael's past. A past that was not only foreign to me, but that also made me tremble with fear.

One particular story made me seethe with anger. I read about how Michael and his dad were walking into a sit-down with their associates in the Colombo family. Both were aware that they might not walk out alive. Unwilling to step into the lions' den without putting up a fight, Michael desperately tried to convince his father to enter the sit-down with guns blazing. Sonny refused. He kept reminding Michael that he had no choice but to accept his fate, whatever it was. And he reminded his son to do the same. After all, it was part of the oath they took when they joined the Family.

I seriously questioned the nerve of his father. What kind of dad willingly sends his son into a death trap? What kind of dad bears more loyal ties to a crime family than to his own flesh and blood? What kind of dad refuses to defend the life of his own boy? I couldn't understand the intentions behind the man.

I continued reading, and my rage got redirected toward Michael. My husband was describing a scene about where his "would-be assassin" was standing. *Would-be assassin? What does Michael know about assassins?* A lightbulb went off in my head. I wondered if perhaps Michael knew this information because *he* was once an assassin or had given orders to one. Either scenario frightened the living daylights out of me.

How did I miss this? I wondered. *Was I that naive, or did I intentionally build a wall to keep me from searching for and uncovering the truth?* To this day, I don't know the answer to those questions.

There was a part of me that didn't want to believe that Michael was "that" man, the kind of violent Mob guy we see glamorized in Hollywood movies. I didn't want to believe my husband was part of a crime family that had a history of murder, theft, and violent criminal activity. But even if he was that man, Michael isn't the same person today. I knew he had made mistakes (he was in prison for a reason), but mistakes don't define who we are. I didn't and would never define my husband by his failings, shortcomings, or poor choices. Lord knows, we've all done some pretty rotten things in our lives, some even not too long ago.

What upset me most from reading *The Good, the Bad and the Forgiven* was that Michael didn't share anything that he wrote in the book with me. I felt that at some point during or after his imprisonment, he could have shared with me more than he did. When I recently asked him why he never said anything, he told me, "Cammy, I would have. Believe me, I would. But I felt you didn't want to know. Every time there was a book, an article, or a new TV show coming out about my former life, you always refused to read or watch it." He was right. How could he be honest with me when I didn't give him the space to be able to?

When the service was over and I turned the last page of Michael's book, droves of people swarmed out of the sanctuary and lined up around the merchandise table. They kept telling me how great he is, what a marvelous work God did in his life, and what a strong woman I was to stand by his side. I faked a smile and tried to keep my head above the raging waters that made me want to scream, "Um, excuse me, folks. I didn't know I married this man. I didn't know he was that person. I didn't know he did those bad things."

As I started handing out the books that these precious people bought, I heard God speak to my heart. "You reap what you sow, Cammy. Sure, I allowed you guys to be together, but ultimately there are consequences for the choice you made." It was the same truth my mother had religiously hammered into my head.

I made a choice to marry Michael. Consciously or not, with that choice I accepted his past, and now I had to deal with the consequences that stemmed from it. I dealt with him being behind bars, and now I had to deal with my fluctuating mess of emotions about his former life, even the dark and scary parts.

When I travel with Michael, I constantly get approached by women who, for different reasons, have found themselves in unhappy situations. One woman may have fallen out of love with her husband and wants to get out. Another may be dating a man who is on his way to serve a prison sentence, and she's not sure if she should stand by her boyfriend's side. Some are in physically or emotionally abusive relationships. Many times these women blame God or outside forces for what their lives look like.

But let's be honest. The truth is, sometimes we get ourselves in a mess because of the choices we've made. And yes, sometimes we are sucker-punched by a life situation over which we had no control. But most times I believe our lives are colored by the sum of our choices. Take a look at my life. Maybe I should have seen the signs about Michael's past. Maybe I should have investigated him more thoroughly or asked him more questions. But guess what? I didn't. So I had to own my part in painting the picture of the hardships in our marriage.

My point is that we have to be careful in making the right choices and accepting the responsibility for the consequences they might have. If you are dating an alcoholic and end up marrying the guy, don't be surprised if your relationship is ravaged by addiction. If you marry a man who has a history of infidelity, don't be mad at God if your husband cheats on you.

But not only that, it's also important to persevere in our marriages, even if we don't feel like it, or the romance is gone, or it gets too hard. After all, we've *chosen* to marry the men we have. Too many people want to walk away from marriage when the honeymoon is but a faint glimpse on the horizon. God doesn't call us to a perfect life or a Hollywood-romance marriage. He calls us to be obedient. When we are obedient to Him and the sanctity of marriage, He will be faithful in working through our union to bring about the good. (If you are in an abusive marriage, however, I am certainly not telling you to stick it out. If you are the victim of abuse, talk to your pastor or a counselor and get help immediately.)

The afternoon I read Michael's book, he had to leave for another engagement. Before he left, however, he noticed I was upset. I didn't have the heart to tell him what was going on in my head. I knew the best thing for both of us was for me to take some time and process the information. I didn't even know where to begin. Late that night, I wrote him a long e-mail, to which he replied with grace, compassion, and honesty.

I learned a big lesson that night. Sure, it was tough (and in some ways still is) being the wife of an ex-mobster, but there was another side to this equation that I was ignorant of. Until recently, I had never given much thought to the sacrifices Michael made to be with me. I didn't realize what he gave up to spend the rest of his life with me. I didn't understand all the things he had risked to love me. I couldn't begin to comprehend the internal battles he had or the danger involved in leaving behind the life. And yes, that ignorance stemmed from me not being fully being aware of his former life, but so many challenges, fights, and difficulties rose from that disconnect.

There've been many times in our marriage when Michael has said to me, "I'm not throwing this in your face, and I want you to know that I think you were the best mom and wife when I was away, but you don't get what I went through to be with you. You get mad about silly things and don't cut me any slack." Granted, since I didn't know about his former life, there was no way I could fully appreciate his life-changing decision. But now it helps to put everything in perspective, and it has changed our marriage for the better.

Knowing Michael's side of the story is what motivates me to be more kind, loving, humble, and understanding in our relationship. And it has left me with a profound sense of respect for the man I chose to spend this life with. My children also get this. If Michael is in a bad mood and my girls hear me complain about his grumpiness, they are quick to remind me, "Mom, if you had to deal with half of the things Dad has had to deal with, you'd be grumpy too." I've got smart daughters.

When Michael was back in a New York prison, I tried to establish a sense of normalcy, but was unsure what that was supposed to look like. Soon I would develop a routine that I would master quite well. There was an art involved in planning the logistics of visiting Michael in the prisons, anticipating his daily phone call, and making sure I was home when he called, and all the while trying to maintain my sanity and care for my family.

Our beautiful condo at the Mirabella wasn't furnished in its entirety, but picking out hand-painted pillows and expensive artwork was the last thing on my mind. I called Sherry and told her, "Continue working on the furniture we've already ordered, and forget about the ones you haven't started yet. We'll make do with what we have."

Sherry was concerned, but it had nothing to do with the unfinished order of custom furniture. She knew that Michael was away in prison and took great care in checking up on me every now and then. Sherry also shared with me how she had a connected (at the time, I didn't know what she meant) family in New York and that her ex-husband spent some time in prison for a white-collar crime. We became close friends, and I looked forward to her phone calls and visits.

As part of his guilty plea, the prosecutors agreed that Michael would serve most of his sentence at Federal Correctional Institution Terminal Island, near Los Angeles. I expected him to immediately be sent back to California from New York. Unfortunately, the pace of the country's prison system is like molasses running downhill. Things take a long time, if ever, to move along. Michael's transfer to Terminal Island was no exception. He was shuffled to three different federal prisons around the country until he got near Los Angeles. He spent time in Lewisburg, Pennsylvania; El Reno, Oklahoma; and Phoenix, Arizona.

I remember visiting him one time right before he was transferred out of MCC. I took Miq with me because I wasn't sure how long it would be before Michael had a chance to see her again. As we stood in line, waiting to get into the prison, a few raindrops fell, moistening my face. In a matter of a few minutes, a heavy downpour crashed down from the sky. I didn't have an umbrella and was unsuccessfully trying to cover Miq's stroller with my coat.

The rain wouldn't let up. It wasn't about to give us any mercy. I was drenched and doing my best to keep my little girl dry. And I was frustrated. Very frustrated. It was cold. We were wet. I prayed Miq wouldn't get sick. And we were waiting for over two hours to get into a prison where my husband was waiting for us. Where he'd wait for us for years. I wiped away the tears that brimmed the corner of my eyes and got on my knees to rearrange my jacket over the hood of the stroller. That's when I noticed Miq's eyes widely peering at me. She sweetly smiled.

In that pivotal moment, I realized that this was our new life. This was the new road we would have to travel. Miq's smile was comforting. It was almost like a confirmation. I felt as if my girl were saying, *Don't worry, Mama. We're in this together. And we're going to be all right.*

For almost eight years, the total time my husband spent behind bars in two phases, my life consisted of prison visits a few times a week when he was at Terminal Island and almost every weekend when he was out of state. Visitation was a complex and timely process, and the more I saw him, the more I realized it was like a full-time job. Michael suggested I hire some help so I wouldn't be inundated with routine household chores while I had so much traveling to do. It wasn't a bad idea.

I couldn't wait for him to get to Terminal Island so that I didn't have to corral my family together and travel to God-forsaken places across the country for long weekends. One of the worst experiences I had visiting him was in Oklahoma. I flew in with my daughter, Sabrina, and Dino, and we arrived in terrible weather. Lightning flashed across the sky. Thunder shook the ground beneath us and made little Miq tremble with fear. Rain poured down in buckets. Even armed with our rain gear and umbrellas, we were no match for the storm and got soaked all the way down to our underclothes.

Before we arrived, I called the place where we would be spending the night and asked the manager about room service. We were flying in late that evening, and I was sure we'd be famished by the time we checked in. The man was kind and told us that while the motel was a full-service establishment, there was no room service. But there was a darling little café around the corner.

When Dino pulled in to the motel, which looked a lot like Bates Motel in *Psycho*, I was on edge. By now I had been to many dingy, scary-looking federal institutions, the kind that make your hair stand up, but this was different. We were in the middle of nowhere. The town was the perfect setting for a 1960s horror movie. There was no sign of a human being. The handful of gas stations and general stores we passed were closed. They were all run-down and sported cracked walls, overgrown weeds, and neon signs that made crackling noises. The streets were dimly lit, and half of our trip to the motel was on a bumpy dirt road, illuminated only by the full moon.

I noticed an elderly man heading our way. He wore faded overalls covered in dust and carried an antique lantern. I couldn't stop staring at the dirt that caked his face and hands. "Howdy, folks," he greeted us with a toothless and friendly grin. "Are you the Franzeses?" (He horribly mispronounced our name.)

The man showed us to our room, and it was horrendous. Dust encased the furniture, and the bathroom looked like it hadn't been cleaned in a few months. I was repulsed by the filth. The Best Western, our only other option, was booked for the night. So unless we wanted to camp out in our rental car—which, of course, no one wanted to do—we were stuck here until the next morning. I'd like to say I made the best of our situation, but I didn't. Dino and my sisters, however, were great sports.

The baby needed some milk, and my brother offered to drive to the diner to find some, but I decided we would stay together as a group. I had stopped grumbling about our unpleasant sleeping quarters, but I was scared out of my mind. I didn't want anything to happen to any one of us. Who knew who or what lurked in this crazy town? Maybe one of the characters from *The Texas Chain Saw Massacre* was hiding out in the woods somewhere. That night, no one slept a wink. We kept hearing undistinguishable noises as our backs pressed deep into the coils of the beds' thin mattresses.

We had dinner that night at Chili's. It took us over an hour to get there because the same weather that greeted us when we arrived in Oklahoma made an encore appearance. As we drove down the freeway in a torrential downpour, eighteen-wheelers flew past us at ungodly speeds, their horns blaring, demanding that we get out of the way. Lightening seared the sky and spooked my girl, but Dino's erratic driving—his only defense to avoid crashing into those crazy, speed-demon truck drivers—was what scared me the most. I kept my eyes shut the entire time.

While my brother and sister were turning even the worst of circumstances into a great adventure, I kept reminding myself that we were here only one more night. The next morning we would see Michael. We had nine or ten hours left in this hellhole. That much I could manage.

That night locusts came out in droves. Talk about random. I don't think any one of us had ever seen a locust in our entire lives. Thousands of these buzzing little creatures swarmed over our motel, our car, and were determined to get inside our room. They kept flying into the air conditioner—with an obnoxious thud for such little guys—to try to find a space they could squeeze through.

While the girls and I wailed in horror, Dino went into hero mode. He tightly wrapped the air conditioner with towels and washcloths, plugging every possible opening with the scratchy cloth. He even used toilet paper to stop up the tiny holes around the windows and doorknobs.

When the sun rose, we expected the nightmare to be over. For Pete's sake, don't locusts need their rest too? But when Dino opened the front door to get the car ready, he gasped and immediately slammed the door. Every inch of our car's surface was littered with locusts. The infestation was still in full swing. My sisters and I looked at him helplessly, and he confidently said, "I'm going to get the bugs off the car. Wait right here, and I'll beep the horn when I'm ready."

I thought. *It's the end of the world. This is what the Bible proph-esied. We're in the middle of a locust plague, and we're all going to either die or be caught up in the Rapture!* I wrapped Miq so tight in her blankets I was afraid I'd suffocate her. I wasn't about to take any chances. I had no idea what could happen from a locust bite or sting. I didn't know if they even stung or bit. My sister and I threw on long pants and long-sleeved shirts, even though it was unbear-ably hot and humid so early in the morning. When we heard the honk, she and I burst through the motel door and flew into the locust swarm at the speed of an Olympic runner. We jumped into the car, slammed the door shut, and assessed any damage. No one was hurt, stung, or bit.

We sat in the car for a minute, while the windshield wipers squeaked their way left and right, scraping away the hundreds of locusts that still were insistent on hanging out on the front of our car. None of us said a word. *Squeak. Squeak.* Another handful of locusts got swept off the windshield. *Squeak. Squeak.* Suddenly, I burst out laughing. This was ridiculous. What kind of place was this? Was this even real? My siblings followed suit. The whole disaster was too crazy for us to be upset by it. All we could really do was laugh.

When I met with Michael that morning, I told him what had happened. He asked the obvious, "Couldn't you have stayed at a better hotel?"

"We couldn't, Michael." I paused for a moment, then stared at him with a poker face and said, "The Ritz-Carlton was booked."

I was relieved when Michael was finally transported to Terminal Island. It would be my second home. The visitation process took some time to get used to. The biggest inconvenience was the endless waiting. Visitors had to wait in a long line outside the main prison doors until the guards chose to let us in. We'd stand in the rain, the cold, the sunshine, and in unbearable heat. And we'd stand there for hours, hoping nothing eventful was happening in the prison that would force the guards to put the inmates on lockdown. For instance, if a fight broke out among the prisoners, visiting privileges were revoked for the day. But no one would tell the women and children standing in line until the last minute, so there were many times we waited only to be told to go home.

The line wasn't the friendliest of places. Most of the women were rough around the edges and looked like they were going to flip out if you so much as looked at them the wrong way. A lot of scuffles broke out, mainly because people were protective over their spots in line. Every time I waited to see my husband, I heard a combination of "Who's standing here?" "You move, you lose your place." "You just got here; get in the back of the line." "Sorry, you moved three inches to the left. You forfeit your spot." The women guarded their positions as if their very lives depended on it.

And no way were you able to take a potty break. If you left, you risked losing your place. Sometimes it wasn't worth relieving yourself because of the extra time and hassle it took—walking back to the parking lot to your car, driving a few miles to find the nearest bathroom, driving back to the prison, finding another parking spot (usually farther away than your original spot), and getting back at the end of the long line. I never felt comfortable asking a stranger to hold my place in line while I ran to take one of my kids to the bathroom. I once asked a woman if she could do me that favor, and she answered me with a silent stare. I assumed that was a no.

In hindsight, I can understand why the ladies seemed hard-shelled. Most of these women worked full-time jobs, had children who always came with them, and had significantly more difficult lives than I had. I was blessed—and never once did I take that for granted—that I didn't have to work or worry about where I was going to get gas money to see my husband. Life wasn't easy for these women. They were probably just exhausted and overwhelmed by the stresses of life, including having a husband or boyfriend behind bars.

Through the years, I noticed the line dwindling. Many of the regulars I had seen the first day I came to Terminal Island stopped coming. I expected that. Things happen. Many women get to the point where they give up. Continuing a relationship with a spouse in prison is a lot to handle. It's definitely easier to tell your significant other, "I quit. I give up. You handle yourself in here, and I'll take care of myself and live my own life out there."

I heard the talk in the lines. This woman needed to pay her bills. That woman needed to find a babysitter. This one was on the verge of losing her house. That one was on the verge of losing her mind. It's not an easy job to support a loved one in prison when the world doesn't stop moving.

I was blessed to have met two wonderful women in line, Lisa and Roni.

Lisa was a beautiful, stylish woman who worked as a personal shopper at Bloomingdale's. Her husband, Josh, was from Israel and was locked up for a drug-related charge. She approached me one day on the line, handed me her business card, and sweetly said, "Hi, there. I see you have great taste and love fashion. I work at Bloomingdale's. If you ever need anything, give me a call." We quickly became friends, and she became my personal shopper. After we visited our husbands, we'd head back to her car, where Lisa had five or six shopping bags full of clothes for me to rummage through. "Take what you want and return the rest," she told me. I never returned a single item.

Roni and I connected because of our passion for dance. She was a waitress who had just moved to California from Canada to pursue a career in the entertainment industry. She stayed on the line for about a year and then left. Roni is one of my best friends today and is my daughter Amanda's godmother. She was an amazing friend during this time and also the second time my husband went to prison. Roni was always there for my children and me. She even let my girls take dance lessons for free at her studio when they got older.

Throughout my journey of raising my children while my husband was away, a handful of people in my life supported and loved me in ways I could never repay. Thinking about Roni and Lisa brings these special friends to mind. I think about Gene and Sandra, the couple who owned one of the homes we rented. When Michael was sent away the second time, I had a tough time making the payments. They let my family stay in the house for more than a year, rent-free. The Kapitans were amazing people who showed us compassion and love. I'll never forget their kindness.

I think about Moshe Diamont and Mark Damon, Michael's business partners, who were good to us financially and supported us when my husband was away.

Bob Shultz, my husband's dear friend who worked on *Knights of the City*, was one of the most amazing men I ever met. He was there for me for whatever I needed, even for things most people would think were so simple, like balancing my checkbook. When our bank account was full, I never thought to reconcile the statements. Bob showed me how.

So many names and acts of kindness come to mind as I write this book. People who mean the world to me, those I'll never forget and will forever be grateful for.

Roni especially was my anchor during this time. We supported each other because each understood what the other was going through. When I was down, she lifted me up, and vice versa. She saved my spot in line if I needed to take a bathroom break. We even had "double dates" and sat with each other's men (Roni wasn't married; she visited her boyfriend) during visitations.

While most of the guards I met along the way were cordial and polite, a few had chips on their shoulders and weren't generally respectful of others. Sometimes they would even carry their resentful attitude over to the visitors. This happened to me on one particular occasion.

That day, I was wearing a knee-length leather skirt and a white silk blouse underneath a blazer. One particular guard spent a minute slowly and methodically staring me up and down and decided I couldn't go into the visiting room because my blouse was see-through. I thought he was joking. There was absolutely nothing see-through about my blouse, and anyway, most of it was covered by a wool jacket. But what could I do? I certainly wasn't going to incite a verbal spat with a guard. I gathered my things, frustrated for having wasted two hours of my day, and walked toward the door of the processing area.

Another guard who happened to know Michael very well watched the entire scene. Before I had the chance to walk out, he jogged over and touched me on the shoulder. "Hi, Mrs. Franzese. I saw the whole thing. Don't leave just yet. I'll get you in to see your husband. Wait right here."

As I stood against the wall, waiting for the fiasco to iron itself out, I noticed the first guard giving me the evil eye. I looked away and focused my attention on the clock. After a few minutes, the mean guard left the room. When he came back, he walked toward me. His eyes blazed with fury, and his nostrils flared. This guy was ticked off. He got right in front of my face, so close I could smell his cheap aftershave.

"Okay," he growled in low and firm voice. "You can go in." He sleazily looked me up and down again. "But don't ever wear anything like that again."

I nodded. *Whatever you say*, I thought and pinched myself to keep from rolling my eyes. My outfit was nothing but modest—any five-year-old could see that—but this guy either had an ego problem, an unhappy life, or he was picking on me on purpose. I later found out he hated Michael. Go figure.

When my husband came in the room, he was fuming. One of the friendlier officers had told him what happened. The last thing I wanted was for Michael to spend the precious little time we had together being upset. Without him saying a word, I tried to calm him down. "Forget about it, Michael. Let it go. It's over. We only have an hour." But he didn't. I should have known better.

Michael motioned for one of the officers and asked him to find the lieutenant. This man in charge happened to be one of my husband's biggest advocates at Terminal Island. The game within the prison walls was, "Treat the guards with respect, and they'll treat you, the prisoner, the same way." If you didn't give the guards any trouble, they were nice to you and even looked the other way when the situation called for it. Because Michael always conducted himself as a gentleman, he was well liked by most of the guards. He treated everyone with respect and, most of all, kept a low profile.

When the lieutenant came over, Michael turned to me and said, "Cammy, stand up.

"Lieutenant, I need you to look at my wife . . . just not for very long," he said, addressing the man again. "Is her outfit inappropriate in any way?"

The guard quickly glanced at me from head to toe and shook his head. "Not at all. Her clothes are fine. Your wife is always well dressed and classy. We've never had any problems with her." Michael shared with him how the other guard had kicked me out in a dramatic display of his power over Michael.

The lieutenant responded, "Don't worry, Mr. Franzese. I'll handle it." Not too long after our sit-down with this kind officer, the power-hungry guard was removed from his position.

Our little girl Amanda was born on January 22, 1987, when Michael first got to Terminal Island. It broke my heart that he wasn't present for the birth because he was in jail. He fought tooth and nail to get a two-day pass to come home, but the authorities refused to grant him leave; Michael was considered too high profile of an inmate.

I arrived at the hospital at the very last minute, in time to give birth. I had been in labor with Miq for over twenty-four hours, so the last thing I wanted to do was sit in a hospital, counting contractions. As soon as my mother and I arrived at the emergency room, the nurse told me it was too late for an epidural; my little girl was on her way. She arrived three short hours later.

My mom was with me in the delivery room, and when little Amanda came shrieking out, my mother shouted, "Oh, Cammy, it's a boy."

Clearly, she was wrong. I was recovering from the worst pain of my life and was in a slight daze with my arms reaching out to hold my little boy when my doctor made the correction. "No, Cammy." He laughed. "It's a girl."

It was a bittersweet moment. Cradling my baby girl in my own arms made time stop and trivialized all the stresses in my life, but there was a notable absence in the room—Michael. I missed him, and I knew his heart was breaking at that very moment over not being a part of welcoming his daughter into the world.

I went to visit Michael a few days after Amanda joined our family. He wanted me to come see him after the delivery, but I knew that wasn't going to happen. I had just naturally delivered a child. The pain, even after a week, was horrible, and I needed a few days to recuperate. It hurt to sit, to stand, to do anything. Factor in my nursing responsibilities, and I was physically having a rough time. But I finally pulled myself up by the bootstraps, mustered up the energy, and went to see my husband.

The sky was overcast, and a light rain showered over the prison. It took me twenty minutes to get there that day, which was an anomaly. Traffic in Los Angeles is as bad, if not worse, than its reputation, and a fifteen-minute commute could easily translate into an hour-plus ride. As I was standing in the rain, feeling tired and achy, I realized I didn't want to be standing there. I wanted to be home with my girls. I wanted to be cuddled up with them in bed. I wanted to relax and give my body a break.

But I didn't entertain those thoughts for very long. I'm glad I didn't turn back and go home, because Michael and I had one of our most special bonding moments. And though we couldn't hug or physically connect to celebrate the birth of our daughter, our hearts meshed on a meaningful level. It was a reminder to me of how much I loved my husband. I finally brought Amanda to see her father when she was about a month old. Michael affectionately dubbed her a "little chicken" because she was long and lean, the exact opposite of Miq as a baby.

While Michael was at Terminal Island during this time, I visited him every weekend and two or three times a week. I didn't always bring the kids with me. It wasn't conducive because of the time I spent waiting. And besides, the entire process was incredibly draining. I loved seeing Michael. The thirty minutes or an hour we were together made up for the hours spent driving, parking, and waiting. But with kids, it was a lot harder. They were quick to get restless and cranky. Most times, keeping them entertained was more of a challenge than I could handle. When they got older, however, they looked forward to visits with their dad like a trip to the toy store. I made sure to take them once a week.

While Michael was in prison during those long years, he made a point of keeping in constant communication with us even outside of the weekly visits. He wrote each child a letter every day and sent handmade cards on their birthdays and on holidays. He didn't want what happened in his family to happen to us.

When Michael's father went away to prison, he had all but cut ties with his family. For Sonny, keeping a connection with his family was a challenge. The policy back then was that prisoners were only allowed one three-minute phone call a week and one eight-hour visit a month. That's not a lot of time to stay in touch with your family. As a result of these stringent rules, Sonny became estranged from his loved ones. He didn't want that to happen, but it was inevitable. It was a shame, really, but the prison system basically forced Michael's dad (and the other inmates) to cut ties with their families.

Sonny's prison experience scared Michael. His worst fear was that our family would drift apart the same way his had, and that our marriage would collapse. When Michael served his time, thankfully, the prison system rules relaxed and more contact was permitted between prisoners and the outside world. My husband used that to his advantage and did everything in his power to make sure he always stayed in touch with the kids and me. He never let his time in a six-by-eight cell or even the years he spent in the hole keep him from reaching out to us in some fashion.

I didn't tell my girls that Michael was in prison until they were older. When they were younger, I explained to them that their father was away at college and would be there for a long time. They were always anxious and excited to "see Daddy at school." Miq quickly caught on to the truth when she started to read. One day, as we were sitting in the visitor area, waiting for Michael, she turned to me and said, "Why would you have a weapon at school, Mommy?"

"What do you mean, honey?"

She pointed to a sign on the wall. "It says 'Leave your weapons.' Why do you need weapons in class?"

The school excuse had run its course. I knew I had to tell her the truth. I explained the same thing to all of my kids when they were old enough. "Daddy made some mistakes a long time ago. He's starting a new and better life right now, but he has to pay for what he did. When he comes home, which will be soon, things are going to be different for Daddy."

They accepted the truth better than I expected and didn't ask any questions. It's amazing how well kids can handle reality much better than a story adults make up to shield them from the truth. My children clung to the fact that they regularly got to see their dad and spend time with him. Even if it was for a little while, in a room packed with twenty other inmates and their own families, my children adored their daddy time. Mistakes or not, they loved him and cherished every moment they had with him.

8

A New Kind of Life

My life was settling into a routine. When I say "routine," I mean trying to balance being a mother of two children with traveling to a federal prison up to four times a week. If you're a mom, you understand that having children pretty much guarantees that you can't plan your day to a science. Most times, you can't even plan your day.

There were times when life on the home front was nothing but a circus. One child was teething; the other was cranky. One was hungry; the other one tired. One was sick; the other one couldn't stop crawling through the house. So having to juggle their needs and my husband's needs was a challenge. There were times I got overwhelmed, especially concerning child emergencies.

When Amanda was six months old, she got very sick. My little girl didn't have obvious symptoms, like a runny nose, a fever, or cough; she just seemed so tired all the time and didn't want to eat. All she did was lie in her crib, staring into space without exerting even an ounce of energy to smile, laugh, or even cry.

One night the girls and I were having dinner at Pina Gambino's house in Beverly Hills. Pina is the wife of Rosario Gambino, a relative of Carlo, the infamous and former Mob boss of the Gambino family. Rosario also happened to be Michael's cell mate at Terminal Island. We met when their family was moving from Brooklyn to Los Angeles to be closer to their father in prison. I showed them around town and helped them find a place to live. Over time we became so close that we ate dinner together two or three times a week. We were like family, and I was thankful to have them in my life at that time, because we helped each other get through some difficult times. They were one of the most devoted families to each other that I have ever met.

The fabulous host that she was, Pina had laid out a feast on the dinner table that belonged on the cover of some fancy cooking magazine. As we indulged in delicious food and good wine, Pina quietly left the table and went into one of the bedrooms where little Amanda was sleeping. When she came back, she looked worried.

"Camille, I'm concerned. Amanda looks real weak. I think you should take her to the hospital."

I dropped the fork I was holding, and it clattered down on the china with so much volume it startled me. When I ran into the room and saw my girl, I froze. Amanda looked lethargic. She was a beautiful baby, but she looked like a lifeless doll, her chest barely lifting out from her body.

Pina's daughter Sylvanna drove with me to the emergency room at Cedars-Sinai. I panicked the whole way there, wondering why I hadn't taken Amanda to the doctor before. Wondering what was wrong with her. And even wondering if she was going to make it. All those questions were cluttering my head and making it impossible to stay sane as I sped down the busy streets, trying to avoid red lights and cars that got in my way. My girl was such a quiet baby. She never fussed, so it was hard to tell if something was wrong. Had she been a crier, like Miq, I would have immediately suspected a problem. But Amanda barely let out a peep if she was uncomfortable or sick.

As I zoomed past cars in an unrecognizable blur, I heard Sylvanna whisper from the backseat, "Amanda's not looking good, Camille. I don't think she's breathing." I gunned the car even more, maneuvering through traffic like a pro and praying there weren't any cops around. I had only one thing on my mind—Amanda. I was going to get her to the hospital as fast as possible, manic driving and all. As I drove, I prayed. Words didn't come easy because my mind was racing faster than my thoughts, so I repeated, *Lord, please let her be okay.*

I finally peeled into the emergency room entrance and hopped out of the car, bundling Amanda in my arms. I ran through the tiled hallways, yelling, "Please help my baby. She's real sick." The triage nurse took one look at my barely breathing daughter and rushed her into a room where doctors were immediately called in. I stood in a corner while men and women in white coats poked and prodded at my baby. As tears streamed down my face, I couldn't help feeling so alone. I didn't even have any time to call my mom. When I caught a glimpse of the needle the doctors were just about to plunge into her back to check for fluid in her spine, I almost passed out. I wanted Michael. I needed him here with me. I missed my husband.

It turned out Amanda had a lung infection and was severely dehydrated. She stayed in the hospital for a week and recovered beautifully. Miq and I never left her side for a second. We crashed on a cot right next to her hospital bed. My daughter's physician, Dr. Pivko, said she was a strong little girl. He got that right. Some things never change. Amanda still is. She is a fighter in every sense of the word.

When Miquelle was three years old, she accidentally locked herself in the bathroom when I was on the phone with Michael. She couldn't unlock the door. I tried everything short of breaking down the door to get her out, but I couldn't. As she wailed and sobbed and complained of being hungry, Michael and I desperately brainstormed by phone about safely extracting her from the bathroom. I called security personnel to help, but even they couldn't open the door.

Five hours later, I was beside myself. I slid my daughter crackers under the door so she could at least have something to munch on, and I patched in the fire department on the line with Michael and me. I felt silly making a 9-1-1 call to free my daughter from the bathroom, but we didn't have any other choice. Finally, firefighters showed up ready to rescue her.

I told Miq, who was still sobbing between bites of graham crackers, to sit in the bathtub and stay there while the nice man came to open the door and get her out. I also cautioned my daughter not to worry, but that it would be loud. The nice man who saved the day was a six-foot-six giant. He looked like the Incredible Hulk with a tight T-shirt and gray firefighter pants. I know the sight of him—his beastly muscles, and especially the ax he slung over his shoulder—intimidated my daughter at first. I'm sure of it because he intimidated me! But giant or not, when Miq realized he had come to her aid, her tear- and crumb-smeared face lit up, and she ran into my arms.

Michael stayed on the phone with me the entire time. This was one occasion when his fellow prisoners showed him some grace and didn't give him any grief over using the phone for longer than his allotted time. Just another day in the life of the Franzese family.

While my world orbited around juggling my kids and my husband, Michael's world revolved around me visiting him and him calling me twice a day. On one hand, we were fortunate to be able to have that constant communication and connection, but on the other hand, it created many tense moments. Michael couldn't fall asleep unless he talked to me at least once a day, and he didn't have the luxury of scheduling these calls at his or my convenience. His phone privileges rested at the discretion of the guards. They decided when to make these allowances. It could be nine in the morning, two in the afternoon, or eight o'clock at night. Not only that, but Michael had to wait in line with the rest of the prisoners to use the phone. We never knew when he'd call; we just knew he'd call.

During his first term in prison, my days outside of home were spent in a mad rush. I was rushing to the doctors, rushing to the grocery store, rushing to the dry cleaner's, rushing to the post office, rushing to the pharmacy, and rushing back home, just so I wouldn't miss his phone call. There were many times I'd have my family over for dinner, and after cooking a huge meal and finally taking a seat to enjoy some food with my loved ones, the phone would ring. It'd be Michael, and I'd have to excuse myself for thirty minutes, missing time with my family.

Every now and then, the dinnertime phone calls would bug my family. "Can't he call back?" they'd ask every time he'd call. No. Michael couldn't call back. It wasn't that simple. Yes, it was inconvenient. And yes, it was annoying. But it just happened to be our world. It was the best he and I could do given the circumstances. Frankly, I felt bad for Michael. Most days, he stood in line for two hours, hoping he'd be able to reach me (which he did nine times out of ten, by the way).

I'll be honest. There were times I got frustrated. I could never mask my feelings well in front of my husband, and Michael was always able to sense my irritation. One day he told me, "Cammy, sometimes it seems you don't want to talk to me."

I sighed. "It's not that. I love talking to you. It's just hard to balance a normal life with running around like a crazy woman to get home and wait for your phone call."

"I get it, but you don't know what I went through to get to the phone." *Neither do you*, I thought.

This phone-call debacle was hard on both of us. Neither of us was at fault; it was a lose-lose situation. Michael had a lousy situation in prison, and I had a lousy situation at home. The two worlds collided many times, and the only way to get through it without one of us blowing up or becoming resentful was with a lot of God-given grace and understanding on both our ends. Believe me, it wasn't easy.

Ironically, today my husband admits that perhaps he was a little too paranoid. He was definitely worried about me and wanted to make sure I was home with the kids and not somewhere I shouldn't be, according to his imaginative mind. Now, as a mother of two children, I don't know where he expected me to be except places that mothers of young kids would be. I certainly wasn't out gallivanting on Sunset Strip or checking out the hottest nightclub.

Michael wasn't just unnecessarily paranoid about my whereabouts; he was also very jealous. Not only did he want me to stay home and wait for his calls; he always wanted to know what I was wearing (and not in a fantasy kind of way, if you get my drift). Our conversations about my choice of dress went something like this:

"Are you wearing short sleeves or long sleeves?"

"What kind of question is that?"

"Short sleeves are too sexy. I don't want you looking too pretty and having every man staring at you and thinking things about you that he shouldn't be thinking."

"Are you nuts?"

"And you better not be wearing tank tops and shorts. Those are out of the question!"

It may have been cute in the beginning—you know, your husband wanting no eyes on you but his—but after a while the behavior bordered on psychotic. Practically speaking, it gets real hot in California. There was no way I was going to run around doing errands in sweatpants and a sweatshirt to purposely look like a plain Jane so as to not attract male attention.

Michael was overbearing in this regard, and it caused a lot of stupid fights between us. Looking back, I can see where he was coming from. I'm not saying he was justified in having a say in what I decided to put on in the morning, but I can appreciate his perspective. Michael was in prison and had absolutely no control over anything, not even when he was allowed to get some fresh air or when he had lunch. The only aspect of his life over which he could exert control was our relationship, and particularly what I wore. After a while, I got used to his possessive side (not that I spent the summers covered up like a nun) and learned to deal with it without piping up and making a stink that would inevitably lead to an argument.

The one area of our lives that was absent of fights or problems was our finances. During his first prison term, we had a lot of money. I didn't know where it came from, and I didn't know exactly how much we had. I just knew we had an endless supply. So I did what any bored mother and housewife would do. I spent it.

I gave my family money. I gave my friends money. I visited my grandmother one day and bought her a new living room set. I loved spending money on cars. Ever since I bought my first Firebird and fell in love with her, I developed a penchant for fancy roadsters. At one point, I owned a yellow Cadillac, a 560 SE, a 560 SEL (because one Mercedes isn't enough, of course), and a Porsche 911 Carrera. These frivolous and usually impulse purchases were silly because I didn't even get to drive these beauties around; I had to be home all the time. My siblings were the ones that got the best use out of my passion. They borrowed my cars to go to their proms, special events, road trips, and even to the mall.

Would you believe I even had a car guy? I'd call up Larry, whom I never met in person until Michael got out of prison, and say, "Hi, Larry. It's Camille Franzese. I just saw a yellow convertible Cadillac at such-and-such place. I want it. Can you get it for me?" And just like that, the next day there was a brand-new, yellow Cadillac convertible sitting in my driveway.

I wish I'd had more wisdom. Instead of driving down the road and asking Larry to fetch me whatever pretty car tickled my fancy, I wish I had saved the cash for a rainy day. I wish I would have known that money, even from what I thought was a bottomless reservoir, would one day run out. But Michael didn't want me to lack for anything. He kept telling me to buy whatever I wanted and he'd sort it out when he got back. I believed him and did as he wished.

Spending stupid money on cars was probably my biggest vice. Despite my stress, I wasn't on any medication (illegal or otherwise), and I didn't drink to cope with my problems. My one indulgence, whenever I had a bad day, was a pint of strawberry Häagen-Dazs and a box of Pepperidge Farm cookies. Those two treats soothed me, even if it was only for a few minutes.

Michael stayed at Terminal Island for more than three years. And for three years I kept the routine of watching my babies, spending time with my family, visiting Michael a couple of times a week, and staying home, waiting for his phone calls. That was my script, and I had it memorized by heart.

We tried to get passes so Michael could be released from prison for a few hours and come home, but we didn't have the best of luck (though he was able to get one later down the road). So Michael and I got involved with Prison Fellowship, the ministry founded by Chuck Colson, to help us with our requests. At the time, they were closely working with the prison institutions to offer furloughs to eligible inmates.

We applied for this opportunity but had to meet some requirements that included a visit to the inmate and his family, as well as a thorough interview. The experience was nothing I had imagined it would be like. I expected to sit down with some spiritual leaders from this group and talk about Michael being nonthreatening. I was also hoping they would spend time with me in prayer. I was wrong.

Two men from Prison Fellowship came to the house one day and for one hour hammered me with questions about the validity of Michael's faith. "How long has he been a Christian?" "Does he pray? How often?" "Does he read his Bible? How often?" "How do we know he is really a Christian?" "Are you really a Christian?"

I'll go so far as to describe the questioning process as "hostile." I didn't get the feeling these guys were coming from a place of love, but of judgment. It would be a different story if they offered to help and were honest about their trepidation in doing so. I'm sure they encountered a lot of inmates who fooled them into thinking they were believers but only wanted to reap the benefits of the organization. I know there are frauds out there, so I could understand their careful concern to best assess an individual's sincerity.

But their tone was caustic and threatening. It almost made me think they hoped Michael was trying to pull the wool over their eyes so they could be proven right. I got pretty defensive. I wanted to fling accusations in their face, questioning them about how Christian *they* were and how many times a day *they* read their Bibles.

Seventeen years later, through Facebook, I received an e-mail from one of the men from Prison Fellowship who had interviewed me. His long-winded e-mail said that for many years he had been bothered by the destructive way he had approached the interview. He asked if I would please forgive him. "I was wrong," he penned, "but I am so thankful that Michael's journey was sincere." I wrote him back and accepted his apology.

It's easy to be judgmental. Especially if you have no inkling of the facts of a particular situation. Sitting on the sidelines and pointing an accusing finger at someone who did this or didn't do that is definitely much easier than sitting back and letting God be the judge. But we're not the judges of any man or woman. It's not our job.

In February 1989, Michael was transferred to a jail in Chicago on some other legal matter he had been dealing with. There always seemed to be another issue for him to overcome as he tried to escape his past. He spent a few weeks there and later returned to Terminal Island, where he was finally released. I stayed in Chicago for about a week and celebrated Easter with him and the kids. Michael's mother joined us. It was one of the few times I was able to spend quality time with her, and I enjoyed every minute of it. We had a blast shopping at Macy's for the girls' Easter dresses.

When Michael was finally released in May, he was home for good, from what we both understood. It was perfect timing. I was pregnant again. Michael had been given a furlough for a few hours, and we took a day trip to the Silver Lake Hotel in Los Angeles. I have a feeling he planned it that way. This was the second time I got pregnant on one of his "breaks."

I couldn't have been more thrilled. Michael was home. We were finally together and could focus on being a family. It was time to restructure our lives with him in the picture. For the first time in a long time, I took a deep breath. I was finally able to breathe easy.

Our big and beautiful boy, Michael Jr., was born on July 15, 1989. We were only a short time away from moving out of the Mirabella and into a home on Burlingame Avenue in Brentwood. The house was gigantic. (We now lovingly refer to the massive house as the "money pit." It chewed an irreparable hole through our wallet.) At 8,000 square feet, it offered seven bedrooms and nine bathrooms. The living room was so spacious, my father used to play baseball in there when Michael Jr. got a little older.

The house was also where Michael's children, John, Tina and Maria, came to visit us for the first time, and both families go to know one another. That time was the beginning of a great relationship that John and I have shared over the years. I think of Michael's son as my own and love him very much. My girls have the same fondness for him and talk to him almost every day.

Michael was beside himself with his new son. Whenever Michael Jr. made a little sound, his father would rush to his side—no matter what time it was or if he was in the middle of doing something important—to check up on him. He did everything for his little boy. He bathed him, fed him, and rocked him to sleep every chance he got.

I was tempted to ask Michael about his prison experience and unearth any details or horror stories, but he never divulged any. I assumed his silence meant he didn't want to talk about it, so I never asked. I figured if he wanted to share anything with me, he'd initiate the conversation. He never did. Bringing up the past would do no good, so I put it all behind me and forged ahead.

The elation of having Michael home trumped the many challenges that accompanied his four-year absence and relieved the heavy burden I had been carrying on my shoulders for a few years. The kids were young and had regularly visited with their father, so after a brief adjustment period, they reestablished a healthy relationship with him. But it took time, and we had to learn how to maneuver through bumpy roads.

The honeymoon phase of Michael being home evaporated when the reality of life steamrolled its way into our new life together. The first few weeks were difficult for the kids. Michael's role as a disciplinarian was new to them, and he shocked them with his mile-long list of pet peeves. Having bad manners was one of them, especially when we were out in public.

At restaurants, Michael would sternly whisper to the kids some combination of: "Don't wiggle in your seat." "Don't finish your drink before dinner." "Stop playing with your food." "Use your inside voice." The girls could barely enjoy their meal without their father telling them to stop doing something. They'd come to me in private and whine, "Daddy is so mean. He's always yelling at us." But soon enough, they got used to his personality and realized that Daddy wasn't mean; it was just how he was.

Finances became another problem for our family. Michael was trying to please us and give us the best life he had to offer. He tried to maintain the lifestyle we were accustomed to, but it wasn't possible. Buying the "money pit," which was one of the worst decisions we ever made, basically dug a financial grave that took years to climb out of.

We bought the house for well under what we were told it was worth, but we also didn't know the troubles attached to buying something so cheap. The plumbing was a constant headache that we quickly found out was impossible to fix. You'd flush the toilet and steaming hot water would come out. The piping system was adequate for maybe a four-bedroom house, not a seven-bedroom monstrosity. All the money we kept putting into the house merely slapped Band-Aids on the structure and continued to burn a hole through our pockets. From the outside, the house looked magnificent. On the inside, it was an expensive joke. Beauty really is skin-deep.

The only good that came out of it was that it was big enough to house my parents and siblings. When we moved in after Michael's release, my parents got evicted from their house. My entire family became our new roommates, and Michael had to support not only his own family, but mine as well. As weeks went by, I noticed that the spark in his eye that had twinkled brightly when he first came home was gone. He was burdened by having to make enough money to support all the growing responsibilities and new additions. I asked him many times about downsizing or saving more money, but his reply was always the same: "Don't worry. Everything is going to be fine. I have everything under control."

I couldn't imagine how difficult it was for my husband. He was not in his element anymore. He had no contacts or associates from New York he could call to get the ball rolling. Once a confident go-getter, Michael was a square peg in a round hole. But he kept a game face on the entire time, acting like nothing was wrong and he was okay.

But let's look at the situation realistically. He had been removed from society for four years. He came back to three kids that he had to establish relationships with. He was burdened by financial obstacles he could barely push out of the way. And he was dealing with creating a new relationship with his wife and kids with his wife's family living under the same roof. Needless to say, the thirteen months that Michael was home with us were nowhere near the glory days I thought they were going to be.

Michael and I also had to shift our individual ways of being to accommodate our new living arrangement: being a couple living under the same roof. We were the same people, but I had created different ideologies and behaviors since being forced to become the sole caretaker of our family and our home. For instance, while he was away, I had turned into the "man of the house."

I was used to being in charge, and Michael was not used to taking a backseat. In the first few weeks of adjusting to home life, I automatically continued to wear the pants, so to speak. When we were out to eat, I'd give the valet person our car keys, order for everyone, and grab the check. At home, I paid the bills, met with the plumber or electrician, and managed the entire household. I couldn't help it; it was like being on autopilot.

Mike would beg me to stop. "It's annoying," he once said.

I think I was as frustrated as he was. "Look, I'd love nothing more than for you to grab the reins. I just need some time adjusting." Soon enough, our roles switched, and Michael felt more in control of his family, a feeling he had longed for since the day he left for prison.

I'd like to tell you the first thing on my mind was Michael and me finally being intimate after so long, but it wasn't. My hesitancy had nothing to do with him or our relationship. I just needed some time to adjust. It had been a long time, and it would take a while to transition back into how things used to be, even in the bedroom.

Michael was so sweet about the whole thing. For the first few days, the kids slept with us. Being able to snuggle up with my husband and my children was one of the most beautiful times in my life. It was a symbolic picture that we were a family again.

Michael and I spent time in prayer about this issue, extended each other a lot of patience and grace, and I focused on what I really needed, to trust my husband and feel safe. And over time, much like every other aspect of our dynamics, our intimacy problems resolved themselves.

We left our huge house after our finances were too big of a mess to sort out. We moved to a smaller house and weren't there for more than a few weeks before we packed our bags and had to move somewhere else. Michael told me he got a better deal in a better neighborhood, but that wasn't entirely true. I didn't find out until years later that the reason we moved the second time since his return was because Michael didn't feel safe. Apparently there was still a handful of people who didn't want him around, to put it mildly.

While he was back with us, we took many weekend trips to Palm Springs. I thought it was strange and silly because we were in such a financial bind, but that was one more thing Michael told me not to worry about. I also found out recently that we took off so much because Michael was getting death threats. There was always someone looking for him, so he was living with us with his head slightly cocked over his shoulder.

The last house we lived in before Michael was arrested the second time reminded me of the O'Hara home from *Gone with the Wind*. The kids loved the house. And Michael was finally getting a steady stream of income working with different Hollywood producers on movie deals. We were finally on the upswing after thirteen months of transitioning, adjusting, and fine-tuning our family dynamic.

November 12, 1991, was a day that rerouted the optimistic course our family was finally traveling. The peace and relative quiet we were blessed with was about to get shattered. It was the beginning of a time when I would change as a woman, a wife, and a mother. I would no longer be the same twenty-year-old, naive Camille Garcia that Michael had fallen in love with.

About six thirty in the morning, I happened to look out the front window and saw five police cars, some unmarked, some patrol, scattered in our circular driveway. About seven or eight men in suits and police uniforms took their positions walking around the property or leaning against the sides of their cars, talking to one another. A few even had their guns drawn at their sides. My heart sank. This wasn't good.

Michael was taking a shower, so I raced up the stairs at top speed to tell him what was happening. I threw open the shower curtain and breathlessly blurted out, "Michael, why are there so many police cars outside?" He looked confused and frightened. "Give me a second to get dressed. I'll be down in a minute."

I didn't want any part of whatever was going on outside. I couldn't even stomach imagining the worst-case scenario. As soon as Michael got to the front door, a forceful knock echoed through-out the downstairs hall.

I didn't hear what the agents said or how Michael responded, I just saw them bully their way into our home. A head detective, who we would later discover was on a long-term mission to put my hus-band away for good, roughly ordered the entire family, including our housekeeper, to gather together in the living room and wait.

We sat there for five hours while the agents and officers dispersed themselves throughout the house to look for what I supposed was evidence. Evidence of what, I hadn't a clue. I just heard them open-ing doors, slamming drawers, turning over mattresses, rummaging through paperwork, searching under furniture and even rugs.

Our kids seemed oblivious to what was going on and seemed content sitting in front of the TV. Miq was six and was the only one who complained about needing to go to school. Amanda, four, was missing preschool but kept quiet, and two-and-a-half-year-old Michael Jr. was mesmerized by the cartoons. Toward midmorning, the waiting was getting ridiculous. The kids were hungry, they needed to go to the bathroom, and they were get-ting restless and cranky. Michael asked one of the agents if the housekeeper could take the kids into the kitchen and feed them. He nodded.

I was done. I was so over this drama and playing the starring role in what felt like a psychodrama thriller. I was angry at the agents for disrupting our home. I was angry at Michael for whatever it was he did that had prompted the agents to disrupt our home. And I was angry at God for allowing this to happen.

I sat on the couch next to Michael and didn't even try to hide my sullen expression. Every time I heard another drawer slam or a pile of clothes get thrown to the floor, I fumed just a bit more. But other than my simmering inner wrath, I kept calm and didn't say a word. Michael kept rubbing my arm and asking if I was okay. I gave him one-word answers to all of his questions. After a slew of curt yeses and nos, he stopped pressing.

Finally, a few minutes after the kids were given permission to go into the kitchen with Ofelia, I abruptly turned to him and hissed, "You gotta be honest with me. Are they going to arrest you and take you away? I need to know so I can prepare the kids. I don't want them to see you in handcuffs and freak out." I should have expected his response.

"Cammy, relax. Don't worry. Everything is going to be fine."

I couldn't handle that pat answer anymore. "Michael. This is not fine. The kids have been sitting here for hours. They're bored. They're hungry. And they're scared. This is not okay."

He tried to grab my hand and continued to whisper, "Trust me, Cammy. Everything is going to be fine."

The ransacking noises were getting on my nerves. My imagination was flooded with futile questions that had no answers and only served to fuel my anger. But I didn't know what else to think. *What are they looking for? What did Michael do? Something had to have happened for them to show up like this.*

About noon, a lanky agent came into the living room and matter-of-factly announced, "Okay, we're leaving now. You guys can come out of the room." I watched the men parade out of the house carrying boxes and crates full of stuff. They confiscated a hodgepodge of items—tons of papers and files from Michael's office, stacks of mail, photographs, even my diaries and notebooks about my early relationship with my husband. I remember one of the agents walking out with a scrap of carpet that we had lying on the laundry room floor. *Why on earth would they take that?*

Michael bolted to the kitchen and got on the phone with his attorney. I went upstairs to assess the damage. Thankfully the house wasn't ransacked, but it was a mess. When I discovered how many sentimental and personal belongings these men had taken from me, I sat on the edge of my bed and burst into tears. It would take close to three years and persistent petitioning of the courts by Michael to get everything back.

Then I thought about the kids. Michael and I had to sit them down and discuss what had happened. This wasn't a normal event that they were used to. They seemed unaffected at the time of the incident, but Amanda recently admitted that day left her traumatized for weeks. She had recurring nightmares that strange men were walking through her house and taking stuff that didn't belong to them.

When I heard the pitter-patter of six tiny feet scurrying up the stairwell, I instantaneously transformed into a tearless, calm, and put-together mother. Nothing good can come out of a hysterical mama. While my two girls quietly crawled on the bed and nestled close to me, little Mikey wouldn't stop talking. "Mommy, are you crying?" His tiny fingers curled around my trembling hand.

I forced a smile. "No, baby. Mommy's okay."

"I know you're sad," he said and rubbed my hand just like his father had done hours earlier.

"But Mommy, they took your stuff, right?"

"Yes, sweetie. And Mommy shed a few tears, but she's okay now, all right?"

My son seemed satisfied with that answer and lay his precious head on my stomach. The four of us lay there for a while. There was nothing to say.

The rest of the day was weird. There's no other word to describe it. I walked around in a daze, numb and in shock. Whenever Michael and I ran into each other, I pestered him with the same questions, "What's going on? Are they going to show up tomorrow and arrest you? I need to know, Michael. Don't keep me in the dark."

Just before dinner and after making a string of phone calls to his attorney, he told me, "John said he's figuring out what's going on.

The only thing he knows is that the feds are investigating something. We don't know what exactly, but they are definitely not going to arrest me." I kept quiet and he continued, "I promise you, Cammy. I give you my word. This is just an investigation." What none of us knew was that it wasn't just an investigation; the fiasco would end up being a parole violation that would land Michael back in prison.

Dinner was quiet. No one made a peep outside of the chews, swallows, gulps, and utensils scraping the plates. I broke the silence. "Are you guys okay? Do you want to talk about what happened this morning?"

Miq and Amanda shrugged their shoulders and kept on eating. Michael Jr. didn't hesitate to pipe up. "Mommy, those guys weren't nice. What did they want? Are they coming back?" Michael took a few moments to reassure them that everything was going to be fine.

After the kids were tucked in for the evening, Michael and I lay side by side in our bed. More silence ensued, apart from the unusually loud ticking of the clock. I was depressed. *What is next? What more do we have to go through?* I wondered.

It was the last night we would spend together for another four years.

Michael was business as usual the next morning. He told me he was going to take Miq to school, run a quick errand at the bank, and said we'd talk more over lunch at our favorite place.

A few hours later, Michael came back. But he wasn't about to take me to lunch. My husband sat in the back of a police car, handcuffed and accompanied by three other unmarked cars. I couldn't believe my eyes. What was happening? It was the exact scenario I had feared. Michael's reassurances were nothing but empty promises. I was reliving a nightmare.

I learned that he had been arrested at the bank, and one of the agents kindly agreed to return all his personal belongings to me. Over the years, Michael became friendly with a lot of federal agents and officers, and to this day I appreciate how kind some of them were.

I couldn't go near Michael. I saw him through the car window. He looked embarrassed and could barely muster the courage to look at me. The agent handed me Michael's wallet and ignored my persistent questions.

"What happened? Where are you taking him?"

"I'm sorry, Mrs. Franzese. I don't know anything." The agent turned to leave. One by one, the police cars exited our driveway like a somber funeral procession. Michael was in the middle car. I watched him go, not knowing when I'd see him again. Not knowing whether this was a legitimate arrest. Not knowing if our three young children would have to spend their entire childhoods without their daddy.

I lost it. I crumpled into a fetal position on the cold marble floor. Ofelia wrapped her arms around me and held me for a while as I sobbed. I felt defeated and broken. All I wanted to do was hold my son, who was upstairs in the playroom and hadn't seen a thing. I lay like a rag doll in the housekeeper's embrace until the avalanche of emotions snowballed to a bearable lull.

And that's when I remembered my choice. I married Michael. It was my decision to spend the rest of my life with him. Whatever happened, this was my life. There was no escape. No running away. No denying. No fairy dust I could sprinkle to make his legal troubles go away. By saying the words "I do . . . for better or for worse," I had agreed to accept the consequences and my circumstances. If he was going away to jail for a long time, there was nothing I could do but with the grace of God walk through my valley step-by-step, day by day.

I gathered myself together and called my parents. My mother answered.

"They arrested Michael." As soon as those words came out of my mouth, my calm cracked. The heaving sobs were back in town.

"Oh, Cammy, calm down. Where are the kids?"

"At school. Mikey's home with me."

"Did anything happen?" I knew she was asking if Michael had done anything wrong.

"Mom, no. I mean, I don't know. I don't have a clue what's going on."

"Okay, try to relax a little. We'll be right over."

My parents spent the next couple of days at our house. That night, my mom took over for me, preparing dinner and giving the kids their baths. They wanted to know where their father was, and I simply said he had to go away for a few days for work. I tried to put on a happy face, but I was drowning inside. I couldn't wait for the kids to go to bed so I could crawl into my own bed and disappear from the world for a few hours.

Michael and I had bought tickets to the musical *Cats*. It was Miq's birthday gift, and she had been looking forward to it for weeks. I couldn't muster an ounce of strength or energy to go. I gave the tickets to my father, "Dad, please. You take her. I can't go."

Mikey slept with me that night. It became a habit that he didn't break for a long time. Having my little boy around was a source of comfort. He helped me collect the strength I needed when I thought I couldn't go on. Without fail, I'd fall asleep to his soothing, little-boy voice: "Don't worry, Mommy. I'm going to take care of you. Everything will be okay." He was just like his daddy.

I didn't leave the house for a few days. I couldn't take a shower. I could barely brush my teeth. I was mulling over what had happened to the point of being obsessed, and the last thing I was thinking about was praying. I was mad. I wanted to grab Michael's neck through those prison bars that had separated him from his family for years and choke him for making this happen.

I needed to verbalize my feelings. For the longest time, I kept my mouth shut and played the role of a "good wife," never questioning, complaining, prying, or nagging. I accepted his reassurances and his promises without blinking, because he, too, had played a role—of a knight in shining armor. He had played it well.

But the knight was beginning to fall off his horse.

Christmas in Terminal Island Federal Prison (1986).

9

Not Again

Finally Michael called from the Metropolitan Detention Center (MDC) in Los Angeles. "Hi, Camille." He sounded tired.

I didn't know how to start our conversation. *"How are you, jerk? I don't like you very much right now."* What if he was innocent? What if this was the government's feeble attempt at trying to play games with him? *Do I give him the benefit of the doubt and feel sorry for him?* "Baby, I'm sorry this is happening. I love you. We love you. We miss our daddy." I took a neutral route.

"You need to be honest and tell me what is going on, Michael."

"Honey, I promise, I don't know. I can't figure this out. I can't even call my lawyer. I'm grasping for straws here, Cammy. I need you to call my L.A. attorney and tell him to work this out."

"What? Are you nuts? I don't want to call him. I don't even know what to say."

He was getting exasperated. "Cammy, just tell him to find out what's going on."

"No. Michael, I'm sorry. I can't do that."

"What's wrong with you, honey?"

I broke down. "I just need you to tell me what's going on. I need you to tell the truth. I need you to think about the kids. I don't even know what to tell them."

"Please don't be upset. I promise you I don't know. The arrest came out of nowhere. No one's told me anything, and I swear I haven't done anything wrong. Don't worry about the kids. They'll be okay. You bring them here next time and I'll talk to them. I'll explain what is happening."

My lips started to quiver, "But Michael, you promised me you wouldn't go away. And you're gone. You promised me!" At that moment I felt like hanging up the phone. And I really wanted to say, "*You did this. You made this happen. And I'm sorry, but I've got to go. I have three kids to take care of.*" But I couldn't. He was my husband. And like it or not, we were in this predicament together.

During the rest of the conversation, his goal was to calm me down with his repeated statements of, "Everything is going to be okay." Who was he kidding, though? If everything truly was okay, he wouldn't be talking to me on a prison telephone. He'd be with me and our children at home. That night, he was shipped back to New York.

It took me a good month before I could wrap myself around the mess and pick up the jagged pieces of our turbulent life. My mother was instrumental in this process. She encouraged me to join her every morning for devotional time. I was quiet as she read the Bible out loud, but it did give me the comfort I needed. When I was ready, I started praying and having quiet time on my own.

But for the first few days and even week or two, my mother graciously allowed me the space to be angry, sad, and bitter. She knew at some point I would have to come to a place of peace on my own—which I did—but in the meantime, she did what she did best: pray. Because deep down in my mother's heart, she knew that not even her optimism and cheery attitude was going to save me. But prayer would.

About a week after his arrest, Michael called me from New York and finally gave me the facts. He was reluctant in sharing the information, but knew he had no choice. Michael was accused of violating his probation. The worst part was, as a result, there was a strong likelihood of him having to serve the balance of his entire ten-year sentence. "I'm sorry, Cam," he said, "but I'm going to have to spend three or four more years in prison, maybe even six." Michael told me the probation violation was prompted by his unwillingness to cooperate with the federal authorities in New York against his former associates. I know they wanted him to. The authorities would visit with him frequently in that regard.

I remember one night when Michael was actually picked up at the house and escorted to New Jersey by the FBI. He told me they wanted him to testify for the government in a big case against one of his former associates. He told me he didn't want to and that he didn't feel it was his role in life to put people in jail. I know he really labored over this. It was a real struggle for him. He wanted to do what was right to convince the authorities that he would not return to his former life, but he didn't feel that turning on people he'd once called his friends was the way he should go about it. When he returned from New Jersey, he told me he did not testify and that the authorities in New Jersey were very upset with him. Within weeks of that incident, Michael was arrested.

As he continued to apologize, I nervously played with the antennae on the cordless phone and zoned out for a minute. We had just hung our Christmas decorations. White lights and fluffy red stockings lined the fireplace, and our ornate tree, blanketed by snow sprayed from a can, blinked with multicolored vigor. *Four years, he said. Maybe six. I'm tired. I'm getting too old for this nonsense.*

"I'm sorry, Cammy. I'm so sorry. I did not expect this setback."

"I don't know what you want me to do. I don't know what I'm even supposed to do. I gotta be honest, Michael. I'm a mess." I was partially upset because our finances weren't as stable as they had been when he went to prison the first time. Since he was back, Michael had been working his tail off just to make ends meet and maintain our lifestyle. Now what?

"Are you okay?"

"Stop asking me if I'm okay."

Years later, Michael told me that that was the day he felt I left him. Not physically or even in spirit, but a part of the old Cammy—the trusting, naive, unquestioning, accepting part—disappeared to never return. At that point in our relationship, I felt that he lost some credibility with me. The trust that we had established over the years was finally showing cracks.

That experience was the first out of two that changed who I was. It turned me into a different woman, not a bad or bitter one, just a different one. And sure, questions about Michael finally simmered in my head. Questions about his past and his connections with his associates back home. Was he part of what they called "organized crime"? Nah. It was impossible. Those people were violent, and Michael wasn't a violent man. They were into drugs, and Michael hated drugs. Those people were murderers, and I couldn't possibly believe that Michael would kill anyone. But for a minute or two before I turned off that disturbing channel in my head, I wondered if it could be true.

Meanwhile, the kids were dying to see their father. When I finally told them that he was going away again for a while because of something bad that he did a real long time ago, their first question was, "When do we get to visit him?" They knew the routine well. Visiting Daddy was like a wild escapade, and they couldn't wait to get back into the swing of things. I, however, could.

Christmas Day was depressing. My family came over, and we had a huge dinner. But the long buffet table of delicious food, the belly laughs that came from story- and joke telling, and good, old-fashioned family company could not camouflage Michael's absence. After my children opened their gifts, which Michael made sure I splurged extra money and effort on, they thanked me with hugs and kisses. But instead of occupying themselves with the heap of pricey, colorful, and noisy presents, they huddled around me like a cozy blanket. "Mom, we miss Daddy." *Yes, my babies, I miss him too.*

When Michael's sentence was confirmed, I knew there had to be some changes. Having four years of experience under my belt, I was certain of one thing—the second time around could absolutely not mirror the first time. I couldn't imagine having to rush home, cancel doctor's appointments, be late for school, or interrupt dinnertime because of Michael's daily phone calls and obsessive behavior.

There had to be a balance. It was tough finding that happy place because we were both living a horrible reality. Michael was stuck in a cramped cell for four years, without his wife and children and with his only contact with the outside world being phone calls and visitations. I was at home, dealing with the day-to-day management of raising kids and a household, with a husband in prison, who wouldn't come home for four years. Either way you sliced it, it was an ugly situation.

But with three children on my hands, there was no way that I could handle Michael's possessiveness and overprotectiveness as I had the first time. I told him, "You can't expect me to be the same person I was in the first four years. I can't. Things have changed. I've got three kids. I have more responsibilities. I can't have you questioning my every move or demanding to know what I'm wearing or where I've been or why I wasn't home. It's not going to work anymore." Michael was very understanding and took my message well.

Even with our new arrangement, I still saw him regularly on my own and with the kids. Michael spent a few months in New York before he was transferred to a couple of different prisons, including ones in California. When he was transferred out of state, we made sure to visit every other weekend. My husband maintained his own routine in prison, religiously staying in touch. He still wrote letters, made the kids birthday and holiday cards, and called them whenever he could. And thankfully, Michael's obsession with my clothing tapered off. He finally stopped insisting I wear jeans and long-sleeve T-shirts when it was ninety degrees outside.

When he was in jail, Michael got acquainted with a handful of infamous characters that I had the "pleasure" of meeting on more than one occasion. One became friendly with my son. I was talking to my husband through the glass pane at MDC and noticed that Michael Jr. wasn't sitting on the floor by my purse. I turned my head and was horrified when I saw his little behind planted on the chair next to mine and chatting on the telephone with an inmate.

I started to panic when I recognized who it was. "Michael," I whispered, "our son is talking to Lyle Menendez."

Michael seemed oblivious to my concern. "Oh, that's okay. Let him talk to the guy. Lyle's just waiting for his attorney." At that point, the Menendez brothers were still awaiting trial for killing their parents with a shotgun in 1989. They had not been convicted yet, and Michael, with his naturally nonjudgmental character, firmly believed that one was innocent until proven guilty. He saw no harm in our son talking to a criminal arrested for murder. I, however, was uncomfortable about the whole thing. Especially because as time went by, Michael Jr. looked forward to his visits with his "friend Lyle." The two frequently gabbed because Lyle's attorney was notorious for being late.

One day I went to the grocery store with my kids, and there was a *People* magazine on the stands by the checkout line. The Menendez brothers were on the cover. Michael Jr. yanked my shirt and screamed, "Mommy! Mommy! Look. It's Lyle. There's my friend Lyle." Michael jumped up and down and excitedly pointed to the magazine, attracting a lot of unwanted attention our way. The shoppers who stood nearby shot disapproving glances my way. I grabbed the magazine out of my son's hand.

He went into full-on tantrum mode. "No!" he shrieked. "I want the magazine. I want to see my friend. I want Lyle!!" While he continued to stamp his feet and convulse in sheer agony, calling out for his "friend Lyle," all eyes were on me. I wanted to get out of there, and fast. Michael Jr. cried the whole way home.

While Michael didn't have a problem with his little boy becoming chatty with Lyle, he did have a problem being handcuffed with his fellow inmate. Some of the prisoners would be handcuffed to one another when they went out to the yard, switched cells, or went to eat. For some reason, Michael would always get handcuffed to Lyle. It wasn't that he didn't like the guy; it was just that all the inmates hated the Menendez brothers. (Apparently, there is a code of honor even in prison. Not only do prisoners hate rapists and child molesters; they're also not very fond of people who kill their own parents.)

Whenever he was handcuffed to Lyle, the prisoners assumed he was Lyle's brother, Erik. The men would lash out with death threats. Finally, Michael demanded the guards to stop handcuffing him to Lyle. "Look," he said. "I'm shackled and handcuffed and I can't defend myself if one of the inmates goes nuts and attacks us. I've got enough trouble as it is. Just stop putting me next to the guy." He even told Lyle, "Don't take this personally, but I've got a wife and kids out there, and I don't want to take any chances of anything happening to me." The guards took Michael's request to heart and never again handcuffed him to the famous criminal.

The kids and I loved visiting Michael in Oregon, where he stayed for some time after he left MDC. The air was pure, the scenery was breathtaking, and the prison staff was unusually friendly and accommodating. Michael once introduced me to a fit, attractive, blond-haired man in prison with him. On subsequent visits, while this man waited for his visitor (it was usually an equally attractive woman, a different one every time), Michael and I sat and small-talked with him.

One day Michael whispered, "So, did you know that blond guy is Jeffrey MacDonald?" The hairs on my arm stood up. I had read about this guy. He had been in prison since 1979 for the murders of his pregnant wife and his two young daughters in 1970. An Army officer and practicing doctor living in Fort Bragg, North Carolina, Jeffrey swore by his innocence and maintained that his family was murdered by a group of people high on drugs.

Ever since Michael told me who he was, I couldn't stop staring at Jeffrey in the visitor's room. It was like watching a train wreck. I didn't want to stare, but I couldn't help myself. One time I was getting some coffee and felt the presence of a powerful man behind me. It was Jeffrey. Though he posed no threat to me, I became unbelievably nervous and spilled my coffee. Knowing who he was and what he allegedly had done freaked me out for a couple of reasons. No doubt the crime that landed him in jail was horrific. What kind of person would do such abominable things? It also made me unsettled that Michael had connected with him, even on a minimal level.

As Michael was serving his sentence in MDC, my arrest by Detective Prieto on an early morning in the beginning of 1992 permanently interrupted my routine. It was, as the saying goes, the straw that broke the camel's back. Being dragged out of my home, away from my kids, and thrown in a prison cell for twenty-four hours for absolutely no reason other than to intimidate my husband, made me face questions, ideas, and changes I never wanted to face.

I remember sitting in that cold cell at the Sybil Brand Institute, my mind racing, while Michelle, the inmate across the block, tried to encourage me. I silently prayed. *Why am I here, Lord? Is there a purpose in me being here?* I knew that I hadn't done anything that would warrant my arrest.

Since I was a little girl, I've been a stickler for following the rules and would never even think of breaking or bending them. I'm not saying this to make you think I'm a Goody Two-Shoes; truth is, I'm just too scared of consequences. When I was a teenager, my cousin and I were in a grocery store when she shoplifted a pack of gum. Three weeks later, I was still sweating bullets and couldn't sleep at night. I was petrified that the police were going to show up at my house and take me to jail just because I was a witness to the theft of some Hubba Bubba.

When I was released from Sybil Brand, my dad and his brother Joe picked me up. I was visibly shaken, but my father shrugged the episode off. He was his sarcastic old self, grinning from ear to ear at my "adventure," and cracking jokes.

"Cammy!" He reached out to help me up into his truck. "How're you doing?"

My answers were curt and as expressionless as the numbing shock that shadowed my face. "Hi, Dad. I'm fine."

"Listen to me, Cammy." He feebly tried to dish out some comfort. "You just gotta be strong, okay? That's all you can do. Think about it. It could have been a lot worse, right? Just be strong. Take it in stride."

Take it in stride? He was talking to me as if I were in the third grade and had just lost the fifty-yard dash to my elementary school nemesis. "Dad, just take me home." I stared out the window during the thirty-minute ride home. I saw nothing but a blur of familiar scenery. I just wanted to hold my kids. God only knows what they thought happened to their mommy.

When I talked to Michael the next day, the shock in his voice was palpable. He stuttered his way through apologies and told me the government was using me as ploy to put pressure on him to take a plea on another case and get even more jail time. It's unfair, he said, but it happens all the time.

I could understand the reasoning, and it made sense because I had done nothing wrong, but it didn't take away the anger I felt at having to suffer through something I didn't deserve. Michael begged me to see him. I couldn't. I needed a few days to calm down and take in what had happened. I asked him to be patient with me. "Give me some time, Michael. Give me some time."

He persisted. "When? Can you come tomorrow?"

"Michael—"

"Okay, how about the day after?"

"I'm sorry, I can't. Michael, I'm doing the best I can; I promise you. I just need more time. I'll come next week." The last thing I wanted to do was see the inside of a jail. I didn't want to hear the clanging of a gate as it closed. I didn't want to go through the hassle of being processed. I didn't want to see prison guards decked out in nightsticks, guns, and bulletproof vests. I didn't want to be near anything that even faintly resembled the hellhole I was thrown in for twenty-four hours. But Michael wouldn't let up.

"This weekend, then. Cammy, you gotta understand. I need to see you. I need to know that we're okay."

"I promise you I'm fine. We're fine. Things are fine. I just need a little space; that's all."

I saw Michael a week later. He had asked a close friend of his to accompany me just in case I was still shaken up. When I got to the station where I had to be processed and prepped as a visitor, I noticed the guards were taking longer than usual. They asked for my driver's license and did not return to the counter in their usual five minutes. I had a sinking feeling in my gut that I couldn't explain. *Something isn't right.* Another five minutes passed. I was still waiting. *Maybe the delay has to do with me getting arrested last week.* The thought made me sick to my stomach.

Two police officers walked through the door behind the counter. *Strange. I've never seen cops in this area before.* I noticed they were headed straight toward me, and when they got close enough, one of the officers reached out with a pair of handcuffs and slapped them on my wrists.

"Camille Franzese, you are under arrest."

"What on earth for?" I protested.

"You're under arrest for not showing up in court." *What are they talking about?* I began to argue with them as I tried to wiggle my way out of their strong grip.

"Are you kidding me? Of course I was there. Why would I not go to court and show up here? Do I look that stupid?"

The officers ambivalently ignored my comments. "You have the right to remain silent. Anything you say . . ." I didn't hear a thing after that. The voice trailed off, and I was left to my own imagination as to what this nonsense was about. *I did have a court hearing scheduled a few days after I was initially arrested and, yes, I did appear with my attorney. Was the government doing this on purpose to bait Michael? Were they just using me again as a pawn to get him to talk?*

A few hours later, I found myself back at Sybil Brand, in a cell next to Michelle. She was delighted to see me, not because I was arrested but because of the company. Her voice was music to my ears. "Hi, sweetie. What happened? Why are you here? This has to be a mistake. These people are idiots. Do you need some socks?"

This time I was only there for about seven hours. Michael's friend, the one who had taken me to see him, put in immediate effort to resolve this obvious mistake. He began faxing paperwork over to the courts and communicating with my lawyer. It only took a short time to clear up the error. Even though the system screwed up, I was scheduled for another hearing to put to rest why I was arrested in the first place.

I hated courtrooms. And this time I wouldn't be sitting in the back while Michael was in the hot seat. I was the one who'd be in the hot seat. I was sick for three days before my hearing. This wasn't just Michael's problem anymore; this was mine.

The issue was a faulty deed that apparently had my name on it. I didn't know a thing about it. The State of California was suing Michael and me, so he was also present at the hearing. Judge Judith Champagne, who led the trial of the infamous Hollywood madam Heidi Fleiss, presided that day. As soon as she sat down and started reviewing our file, she seemed a little perplexed about the case. She didn't understand why I was dragged into the mess as a defendant.

Michael was being pressured to take a plea in this case, but he refused. He knew it was a scare tactic and told the district attorney that he wanted to go to trial. "I'm not worried about my wife because she did nothing wrong and the judge will see that." The DA finally caved in and told the judge he was willing to work something out.

Knowing the case was bogus, Judge Champagne offered to give my husband a plea of time served. He agreed under one condition: that I would be cut loose from the case. She told our attorney that if I was willing to plead to a misdemeanor, she would have the case expunged from my record. It would be as if this never happened.

While I didn't want to plea to something I didn't do, Michael believed it was the only thing I could do. He never for a second thought I would be found guilty at the trial, but he warned that if I moved forward, it was going to be ugly and time-consuming. It would take me away from home and the kids. It would also be financially draining.

As hard as it was for me, I finally relented and pled to a misdemeanor. The fact that the plea was accepted was proof that the state had no case against Michael or me. It was an utter waste of our time. I was sentenced to six months of informal probation, which just meant I had to stay out of trouble for that length of time. After the six months were up, the case would be expunged from my record. Normally, it takes a judge about a year from the date of expungement to write a letter clearing a person's record, but in a show of compassion, Judge Champagne, convinced of my innocence, mailed it to me in sixty days. I felt she was on my side from day one.

During this trying time, God brought to light my messed-up priorities. Since I'd met Michael, I had held him above everything and everybody else, including God. My mother used to remind me all the time that Michael was just a man. He couldn't save me from everything. He couldn't protect me from everything. The only man who could do those things for me was Jesus. When Michael and I were getting serious, my mother used to say, "Cammy, I see how both of you put each other first in your life. You have to stop that. You have to put God first. You'll never be successful or at peace if you don't put God ahead of Michael."

It was a lesson that took me a long time to learn. Though Michael appreciates that truth today, when he fell off that pedestal,

I know he took a hard hit. He strove to be my Superman, and when he realized he couldn't perform at that level, he was disappointed, even though he had no reason to be.

Married women especially have to understand this principle. Our husbands will fail us. They will let us down. They will disappoint us. Their failures are usually unintentional in marriages that are solid and grounded in faith. They are not trying to hurt us or cause us pain. Sometimes our husbands simply make mistakes; they are human, after all, just like we are. And when we place unrealistic and unattainable expectations on them to be perfect, to have it all together all the time, and to fulfill our every wish and command, we are basically setting them up for failure.

When our spouses fall, not only do we hurt, but they hurt as well, because they know they have let us down. If you have your husband or parent or boss or even your pastor on a pedestal, take him off. Give God His rightful place in your life. Give Him your heart, even before your husband. Give God your ultimate trust. He is the one who will never leave you or forsake you.

Michael and I have since worked through and resolved the expectations I had for him, and those he put on himself. I think he still feels the pressure to come through for his family because he does take his responsibility as a man, husband, and father very seriously. And he always does his best to do whatever he can for us.

But let's be honest. Life doesn't always turn out the way we want it to, even if we make what we think are perfect plans or are really smart and can find solutions to life's problems. Life is larger than we are. I try and pray daily that I can be the wife who always gives grace and understanding to my husband in that area. I'll be honest. Some days are harder than others. Still, I don't esteem Michael as my savior; I reserve that spot for God. Doing so removes the heavy weight my husband was used to carrying and makes him (and me) rely on God more.

When I was thrown in jail and then had to deal with the aftermath, it practically forced me to rely on God. I spent more time in the Word, searching for answers, learning lessons God wanted me to learn, and seeking my purpose in life. Reading the Bible regularly gave me the wisdom I needed to raise my children and prepare them for life's disappointments. I certainly was not going to allow them to grow up with a Pollyannaish view of life. I also started attending church more regularly. Because the kids were a bit older, it was a little easier to lasso them together and go as a family.

My mom and I spent many cherished hours doing devotions and praying together. I never took for granted her faith values and how much she prayed for Michael and me. I took her example to heart and still pray every day that I have the same heart for and faith in God that my mother had. It was a legacy she lived her whole life and one that I strive to one day leave for my kids.

I celebrated my thirtieth birthday when Michael was away during those four years. The night ended up being much more than a chance to let loose and commemorate a milestone. It was an eye-opening warning about the realities of temptation.

For weeks leading up to my big day, I was depressed. I was spending another birthday without my husband. I felt much older and wiser than I had been in my twenties. I was starting to wonder if my life was ever going to change. I wondered if Michael and I would ever live a "normal" life, one where our lives were intertwined, not lived in phone calls, letters, and one-hour visits. I even started wondering if Michael and I were still going to be in love when he came back.

My friend Roni hated seeing me in that dismal state of mind and rounded up some girlfriends of ours to celebrate my big day.

She wanted to give me at least one night when I didn't have to think about my husband being in prison and me surviving as a single mom. To be honest, I wasn't much of a party girl and begged her to arrange a simple dinner instead.

Roni picked me up and even brought a babysitter, so I couldn't squirm my way out of going out. My girlfriends Nora, Darlene, Molly, and Justine joined the festivities, and we had a lovely dinner at an amazing restaurant. Amid succulent food, glasses of red wine that warmly cascaded down my throat, and being with my girlfriends, away from housecleaning, taking out the trash, and planning my next visit with my husband, I felt all my stresses vanish.

But one glass of wine too many led to an emotional breakdown. My high spirits came crashing down as I stared at my chocolate birthday cake. My crocodile tears glistened in the glow of the candles. "Am I old?" I asked my friends. "Is my husband coming back? Is my life going to be like this forever? Is this it? Is this my lot in life?" They stared at me, unable to answer my questions and not sure what to say. I blubbered a little more until Roni interrupted me.

"That's it," she boldly announced. "We're not going home yet." Then Roni persuaded me to check out one of the hottest clubs in L.A. I went, but I was high-strung and paranoid. Michael had a lot of friends who were always out and about at the hippest places. What if someone saw me? What if they got the wrong idea and thought that while my husband was suffering in jail, I was getting my groove on at a dance club?

My girlfriends didn't give me a chance to entertain my anxiety. They grabbed me by the arm and led me straight to the dance floor. Dancing reminded me of the old days. I loved it. My passion was dancing. So for a few hours, with the music pulsating through our veins, I danced with Molly and Roni until blisters started to form on my feet. I needed a break. Dancing in stilettos is an art that comes with its share of pain.

I took a seat in the lounge, patting my forehead with a tiny cocktail napkin to clear away the sweat. Nursing a glass of ice-cold water, I realized there was a group of guys in front of me. My instinct was to ignore them and look away. I did. None of them seemed to notice me anyway, so I continued to rest my feet awhile and waited for Molly and Roni to get back from the bar. As I waited, looking around the club to see if I recognized anyone, I noticed a tall man staring at me.

He was about six foot three and lean, with dark, wavy hair and a kind smile. Oh yeah, and he looked like a *GQ* model. Definitely more than easy on the eyes. I took one look at him and all I could think was, *Watch out, Camille. You are now officially in the lions' den.* Let me make it clear that I had no immoral intentions that would betray my integrity or the integrity of my marriage. I didn't even want to talk to the guy. I simply recognized his attractiveness. Nothing wrong with that.

Mr. GQ took a seat on the couch next to me, a little too close for comfort. I casually inched away, creating a space I felt comfortable with. He started talking to me. And flirting. He was seriously flirting with me. "So, you here with your friends?"

"I'm here celebrating my thirtieth birthday!" I hoped saying my age would be a deterrent. Maybe it would make me seem like an old lady.

"You're kidding, right? I turned twenty-nine yesterday!"

On one hand, I was amused by the attention. On the other hand, I didn't think I should be talking to him. I excused myself for a moment and went to look for Roni. She had been watching from a distance and told me to relax and have fun. "So, you're talking to a hot guy. Big deal. You're not doing anything else. Stop worrying so much."

The dancing and partying continued, and Mr. GQ wasted no time finding his way back to me. "Excuse me," I said with attitude in my voice. "Did you forget that I'm married?"

He, of course, found it an amusing challenge. "So your husband doesn't mind you coming out late at night?" he asked playfully.

"He's away."

"Away?" Mr. GQ raised his eyebrows suspiciously. "So what nationality is he, anyway? Is he out of the country or something?"

"He's Italian, and he's definitely not out of the country." At that point, my friends had started hanging out with his friends nearby, so they could hear the whole conversation. Every few seconds, they snuck glances at me from the corners of their eyes.

"He's Italian?" Mr. GQ threw his head back and downed a shot. Then he snickered. "Is he in the Mob or something? Is he, like, a big-time, tough-guy gangster?" When my friends heard that, they couldn't help but burst out laughing. I thought Roni was going to split her pants.

I decided to play along. "As a matter of fact," I said, sipping my water slowly, "he is."

But the guy didn't take the bait and instead shot me a smile that would melt any girl's heart (except mine, of course). He leaned in close and said, "I know you can come up with a better line than that."

He didn't get the picture that I wasn't interested, even after I walked away and kept shoving my single, good-looking girlfriends in his face. I never gave him any indication that I wanted to see him after that night. I refused to give him my phone number.

The conversation. The flirting. The dancing. I knew all these things could get any married man or woman in trouble. I knew it could take me somewhere I didn't want to go. It was a recipe for disaster.

Yes, hanging out at a club with my girlfriends and talking to men was like being whisked away to a refreshing world that had nothing to do with courts, attorneys, visiting hours, or legal fees. But I could see how quickly something so seemingly innocent could take a downward spiral into the welcoming arms of temptation. I didn't want to trek anywhere near that slippery path.

When we left the club that night, one of my friends said, "Cammy, see how much fun that was? We have to do it again!" Thing was, I didn't want to do it again. I was a married woman with children. I loved my husband. And I did not want to purposely put myself in a situation where I could make a terrible decision that would threaten my marriage or my family.

It's easy to make a terrible decision when you're in a vulnerable place. Matter of fact, because of the hardship I was in, a woman I casually knew told me I "deserved it." I "deserved" to have a little fun on the side. I "deserved" to take a walk on the wild side. I "deserved" to have an affair. I told her she was crazy and needed to have her head examined.

I had been celibate the entire time Michael was away, and I had no plans to jump ship. I knew full well the ramifications of an affair, so the thought never even remotely crossed my mind. I ignored my friend's persuasions. I believed in my love for Michael. I believed in our marriage. I believed in my commitment. Nothing was going to get in between those things. Nothing at all.

When your spouse is away for a long time—whether it's on a business trip or in prison—and you are alone, you become a magnet for others. In the years Michael was gone, there were many times I was hit on by men, but I knew entertaining even an innocent flirtation or invitation to the coffee shop spelled trouble. Things aren't always as innocent as you would like to believe.

I heard about men and women having multiple affairs all the time. When I stood in line to visit Michael, I listened to the chatter. This one was just dropped off by her boy toy. That one was going to see her new guy after she visited her husband. And don't think the men in prison were immune to checking out the other side. Many of the prisoners were visited by more than one woman. In other words, they had both wives *and* girlfriends, sometimes two or three apiece.

The bottom line is that temptation is out there. And if your marriage is on shaky ground, taking a step forward in the direction of an affair is guaranteed to lead you to one place—destruction. My thirtieth birthday party opened my eyes and reminded me of the importance of being regularly connected to God, because that's what influences and shapes the choices you make in your life. When your spirit is saturated with His, you can see through temptation a lot more clearly than if you were drifting away from Him.

Being connected on a meaningful level in my faith helped me when I was plagued with thoughts that I was too old, that my future was uncertain, that my life was nothing I hoped it would look like. I may have had more questions than answers, but I had a solid faith that somehow, in some way, God would work all things in my life and Michael's for His ultimate good. As always, He was true to His word.

10

Coming Home

If someone had approached me on my wedding day and told me what my future would look like, I would have told them they were crazy. I would have never believed I would have been able to handle my husband being gone for eight years. Or the repercussions that would come from his former life in organized crime. Or the changes it would bring in me and in how I looked at life and even my faith. But when you are equipped with the power of prayer, support from others, and the understanding that life really isn't (nor is it supposed to be) a fairy tale, it's amazing what dark valleys you can walk through.

I also realize now that God will allow us to go through struggles in order to prepare us for His ultimate purpose for our lives. This was certainly true in Michael's life. My husband had accepted Christ into his life before he went to prison the first time. And I believe that acceptance was sincere. However, he never really surrendered his life to Christ. He could not process the thought of "surrendering" to anyone, Jesus included. At the point of his early acceptance of Christ, I believe Michael was too much a product of his former life to fully understand that Christianity is all about selling out to Jesus, giving Him complete control.

It wasn't until Michael was imprisoned for the second time, out of sheer desperation and hopelessness, that he sold out to Jesus and his conversion to Christianity was made whole, in a way that would allow God to truly use him. In his book *The Good, The Bad and The Forgiven*, Michael describes the experience he had the first night he was jailed on his probation violation. How he agonized over the thought of possibly losing me and all that was dear to him. How he was overcome with hopelessness and fell to his knees, begging God to do something to make him feel better. God answered Michael by giving him hope and comfort in the reading of his Bible.

He spent almost three years in solitary confinement for his safety during his second imprisonment, and God used that time to draw closer to him and strengthen Michael in his faith. My husband will be the first to tell you that God needed to bring him to his knees, humble him, and make him know he was not really in control of his life, but that God was. I believe God used Michael's second imprisonment to make him the man of God he is today. His ministry is evidence of that.

In November 1994, Michael was released from prison. He spent a good portion of his sentence near our home, either at the L.A. County Jail or at FCI Lompoc, a minimum-security facility about two hours away from Los Angeles.

On that chilly, late-autumn day, I watched him walk out of the facility and down a long, narrow sidewalk toward our parked car. I was surprised to notice he didn't look excited, but nervous. He moved at a brisk pace and slammed the car door shut after he got in. "Drive," he said blankly, his eyes circling the perimeter of the prison parking lot.

Thankfully, the kids didn't notice Michael's unease. They could not contain their excitement and bounced up and down in the backseat, chorusing sweet shouts of "Daddy! Daddy! Daddy!" Michael later told me the reason why he was acting so strange.

He'd heard a rumor that more indictments were coming down the pike, so when he was released, he was paranoid that the feds would be waiting for him around the corner. He didn't want to chance reveling in his newfound freedom just yet. But besides me and three kids who were anxiously awaiting his homecoming, no one else was waiting for Michael. No feds. No cops. No handcuffs. No men in suits. We were home free. Finally.

Michael wanted to make a pit stop at Wal-Mart. The superstore had just opened up not too far from the prison, and he was beside himself to check out this new phenomenon. Everybody was talking about it. You would go in the store with the intention of picking up an oil filter for your car, but could just as well walk out with a cart full of toilet paper, wool socks, deodorant, a coffee maker, and a shower curtain in addition to the oil filter. Wal-Mart had everything you could ever want.

Michael and I held hands as we strolled through the store, laughing at how our kids hypnotically stared up and down the tall aisles filled with toys and games. They weren't the only ones in awe of all this megastore had to offer. Their dad was mesmerized by the variety of products you could find in just one place—from the plethora of electronics filling one aisle to the abundance of household appliances in another to the glass cases of jewelry in one corner and the sub shop smelling up another corner.

It was almost too much for him. Especially the aisle that showcased cleaning products. When we walked down that row, it was almost like I didn't exist. The thousands of bottles of bleach, furniture polish, disinfectant, mops, and brooms beckoned him with a seduction he couldn't have ignored even if he'd tried. Clean freak that he was, Michael could have spent the entire day and our whole checking account on the new gadgets that promised sparkling floors, greaseless ovens, and streak-free windows. Okay, fine. I'll admit, I was pretty amused and impressed myself.

While the first day having Michael back was a bit awkward (it was weird adjusting again to the dynamic of having a male figure in our tight circle), things transitioned quickly the second time around with the kids. At the time Miq was nine, Amanda was almost eight, and Michael Jr. was five. They were thrilled to have Daddy back for good, and after a few weeks it felt as if Michael had not been away at all. I think the biggest challenge the kids had to wrestle with was sharing Mommy with Daddy.

For the last few years they'd had me all to themselves, and they took advantage of every minute. Even though they had their own bathrooms, they loved to get ready and take baths with me in the master bathroom. Most nights, they'd cuddle up with me on my bed, and we'd watch movies together. With Michael in the picture, they couldn't have all of me all the time. When they began to understand this new dynamic, my kids sulked a great deal. But once Michael and I eased them into the new arrangement, they adjusted fine. They learned to knock before they came into our room, and they learned to sleep in their own beds and use their own bathroom.

With Michael back in the picture, our children had to revert to his interpretation of how well-behaved kids needed to act. The Manners Nazi was back in action. This annoyed not just the kids; it also irked me. For instance, my husband refused to let anyone leave the table unless they had eaten every morsel of food off their plates. I used to tell Michael all the time, "I don't know where you came from, but we don't belong to the clean-the-plate family. When they're done eating, they're done."

He also couldn't believe I let the kids have a choice of what they wanted to eat for dinner. (Granted, I always gave them healthy versions of what they asked for and rarely indulged nonsense requests for ice cream and potato chips.) "No, no, no," Michael would balk. "You tell them what they're going to eat for dinner, and that's that. End of story."

There was no doubt about it; Michael was a tough cookie. He demanded respect. And it wasn't a bad thing. Of course, children need to respect others, especially their parents. But Michael was known for going a little overboard in his need to dictate orders. In my husband's defense, it's how he was raised and how he expected his kids to be raised.

Michael had been an exceptional little boy. Sonny once told me that, growing up, my husband never talked back to, disagreed with, or raised his voice at him. When Sonny said it was time for dinner, Michael was at the table before his dad could get the last word of the sentence out. When his father called his son's name, Michael would drop whatever he was doing that same second and run to his father's side. It was like pulling teeth for Michael to be satisfied with anything less than that kind of obedience from his own children.

A year or two after Michael came back from prison, he cooked a delicious dinner for the family. When he was finished setting the table and laying out all the food, he yelled for us to come down to eat. Two minutes later, none of us were at the table (I don't think we heard him). He turned on his outside voice and roared, "If you guys are not down in five minutes, this food is flying off the table!"

I came down the stairs and started giggling. Unfortunately, that didn't help to calm Michael down. I slid my arms around his neck, which was covered in bulging veins, like the Incredible Hulk's, and whispered in his ear, "Really? You are really going to throw all this food on the floor?" He managed a smile. It was the beginning of him learning how to be a little easier on the kids. I had to remind him many times that he couldn't run this family the same way he ran his Colombo crime family.

Battles erupted in the house because Michael believed his way was usually the right way. It was hard for him to understand that it was okay if someone had a different opinion than he did. Michael and Amanda would argue about everything. My feisty daughter hardly ever agreed with her father. In the beginning, Michael wasn't thrilled that she didn't accept the answer "Just because" or "Because I say so" when she had been told to do or not do such and such.

I, however, had the mind-set that it was good for our kids to share their opinions and thoughts with us, as long as they did it in a respectful way and didn't scream their heads off or use colorful language. Our unique family structure worked well when Michael was in prison because our kids and I had an open and sharing relationship. I believe that is why today they love hanging out and traveling with us, even though they're adults and have lives of their own. That kind of bond between children and parents seems rare nowadays.

There were other opportunities for growth when Michael came back from prison. We had to adjust to his obsession with cleaning and organizing. While we were lucky to have a man in the house who took pride in cleanliness, for the longest time it drove us crazy. Everything had to be in its proper place. If a piece of artwork on the wall was hanging just a half centimeter off center, Michael wouldn't be able to sit still until he angled it just right. He hated seeing dirty dishes in the sink for more than ten minutes, and he'd clear away any glasses that were left on the kitchen or living room tables if you walked away for five minutes (even if you weren't finished drinking).

Michael is so much better about that now and doesn't fidget or get agitated if our house isn't perfect. Smudges on the wall, streaks on the mirrors, and a handful of dishes in the sink don't get him wound up. The girls and I have come to appreciate his tidiness. My husband is a joy to have around when it comes to housework. He doesn't groan or object to pitching in; matter of fact, he prefers it that way. (I'm such a lucky wife!) My daughters always complain that they'll never be able to find a man like their father. And not only does he help out around the house; he also does sweet things for us, like buying us coffee every morning.

For the next few years, we focused on reconnecting as a family. We went to church regularly. We always had meals together. We occasionally took trips. It was a quiet time of re-creating what was lost when Michael was absent from our lives.

The two biggest challenges Michael and I had to sift through when he came back home for good were our much-evolved relationship and our financial situation. He basically returned to a different person. A part of me believed that Michael didn't like the woman I had become. I wasn't the twenty-year-old girl he had first met. I was more aware, more suspicious, and more independent. I had survived about eight years of raising a family and managing a household without my husband's physical presence. And I had done a pretty decent job. I didn't need him in the many ways I once had.

There were some pluses and minuses to losing my soft edge. While the change hardened me in some ways and built around me a wall that was probably too high and too strong at times, my eyes were also open to the realities of life that I had once ignored. I wanted to know what was going on, especially concerning my husband, our finances, and any pending legal trouble. I was through with isolating myself in the shadows. I particularly became attentive to the details of what I was signing and more actively involved in what was going on in our family. I didn't want any surprises.

When Michael went away the second time, the film company he had started doing business with gave me a monthly stipend that barely covered our expenses. Don't get me wrong; I was grateful to have that allowance, but money was always tight at the end of the month. We had to budget very carefully and allow for extra emergency expenses, like the kids' dental visits or an unexpected car repair.

Michael's release put an end to the stipend, and he was on his own to provide for the family. He was still haunted by the pressure of giving us a lifestyle we couldn't afford. He wanted nothing but the best for us, and though I get that, I wasn't interested in a big house, fancy cars, or couture clothes. I just wanted my family together. Looking back, however, I feel I could have done a better job taking some of that pressure off.

Michael had promised me that once he got out of prison, we could live anywhere we wanted. I held him to that promise, but I did so at a high price. I insisted on staying on the west side of L.A., a very expensive place to live, because I didn't want to uproot my children. I should have not been so stubborn in my demand and should have instead compromised on somewhere more affordable for us to set up house.

We endured financial hardship for years, even though my husband was working in the entertainment industry and making deals. I never knew how stretched he felt in his wallet because he never shared it with me. Anytime we talked about finances (which was usually not very often and very brief because he wanted full control of the reins), he'd say, "Don't worry. Everything is fine. I'll get it together. We'll be fine." It was the same vicious cycle he had spun about his legal drama.

Michael finally broke down a few years ago and admitted that we couldn't continue living above our means. We sat down and had our first budget session, or what I affectionately call a "sit-down." I had some shifting to do in my head, as did Michael. I needed to give him the space to make the best decisions for our family, even if it meant moving somewhere so we didn't have to pinch pennies and live paycheck to paycheck. He needed to be honest with me about the realities of our checkbook. So I told him, "I can take it. You're not going to hurt my feelings. If I hear something I don't like, I'm not going to run out of the room like a moody teenager. Let's just get everything out in the open." That day was the beginning of a new chapter in our relationship.

I deeply admire Michael for supporting us the entire time he was away and when he came back. Honestly, I don't even know how he did it. Even though times were tough, my husband worked tirelessly to make sure there were no dramatic changes in our lifestyle. I don't know many husbands who would sacrifice in that way for their families. Michael was committed to providing us with normalcy. He figured that having to deal with his being away for years was enough of a burden for us to shoulder. My husband is a hardworking man, and in his own way, he is my Superman. He always will be.

I got pregnant again toward the end of 1996. When I went for an ultrasound at around eight weeks, my doctor was worried at what he saw. He noticed an abnormal amount of fluid around the baby and told me to come back for another screening in a month. He explained that this type of excess fluid was a strong indicator of the presence of X syndrome, a genetic defect where a female child's second X chromosome is missing entirely or is incomplete.

We left the office, and Michael and I stood on the sidewalk of Wilshire Boulevard. Cars whizzed past in rush-hour traffic, and people hurried by on their way somewhere. I was frozen to the concrete, oblivious to the five o'clock rat race around me. Michael held me tight and said, "Whatever happens, Cammy, we'll get through this."

The truth was, I was scared. Not only that, but I wasn't sure I could handle a special-needs child. I definitely wanted the baby, but I had so many questions running through my mind about what that would entail. Could I handle it? How would the other children react? How would it affect my relationship with Michael? The anxiety I felt rattled my peace.

Four weeks later, the ultrasound showed no sign of life. My doctor believed the baby's heart probably stopped not long after the first ultrasound. I was relieved, and then I immediately felt guilty. Had I caused the miscarriage? Did my questioning attitude have anything to do with this baby not surviving? Was I a bad person for having doubts? Michael was sweet during the ordeal and reassured me that it wasn't my fault. "You were scared. It's normal. You didn't miscarry because of anything you did or didn't do." (Three weeks later, my doctor examined the fetus and told me he found no abnormalities; it was just a miscarriage.)

After the D&C, I stayed in bed for a few days, overwhelmed by sadness and wondering if I would ever have kids again. I didn't feel that our family was finished, but this miscarriage made me wonder if perhaps my feeling was simply that, a fickle emotion of something I wanted that God might not have had in His plans. And so I resolved in my heart that I was content with my three beautiful and healthy children. If our family was officially complete, then so be it. I felt blessed beyond measure.

Two years later, I gave birth to beautiful Julia on August 19, 1998. My sister Sabrina was pregnant at the same time and had her son, Hendrik, a month after Jules came into our world. The two cousins are the best of friends. It was wild (and very comforting) being pregnant at the same time as my sister. We could empathize with each other's morning sickness, back pain, bloating, and fatigue. But we didn't spend our pregnancies complaining about how bad we felt. When one was down, the other picked her up, and vice versa. We seesawed in that same fashion until our babies were born. It's a special moment when sisters get to share pregnancy together.

We had a family trip to Hawaii scheduled a month before Jules was born. Michael suggested we cancel the trip. I thought he was crazy. I was dying for a little R&R and had been looking forward to this trip since it was just an idea I was toying with in my mind. But he begged and pleaded with me. "Trust me on this one, Cammy. I don't think you're going to go another month. I have a feeling the baby is going to come a lot earlier than you think. Let's just go away somewhere close to home. Just in case."

I was disappointed, but I agreed. We stayed at the Four Seasons in Carlsbad for five days and had a blast with the kids. The day I got back from our mini-vacation, I had close to three and a half weeks left before I was due. The nursery was practically empty. I didn't have a crib, a bassinet, or a diaper-changing station and was planning to go shopping with Sabrina. My baby had other plans.

My water broke right before Sabrina showed up, but I didn't let that stop me from trying to convince her to keep our shopping trip as planned. "What are you—crazy?" she said. Michael shared the same sentiment and made me call my doctor. Dr. Leong wanted to see me right away and said that if I didn't go into labor on my own, she would induce me in the morning.

I went into labor that night and was a little nervous because my baby was early. I delivered a tiny little girl with long limbs. As soon as the doctor put her on my chest and I snuggled the five-pound, wet, warm, and wiggly creature in my bosom, a nurse quickly scooped her out of my arms. *Why the rush?* I wondered.

In a calm voice, the doctor told me that our little girl was breathing heavier than they would like her to. A test showed that she had a serious lung infection. I saw her in the incubator, and my heart broke. Her heart was beating unusually fast through her thin, tissue-like skin. But Jules was a trooper. In two days she was back to normal and started eating and gaining weight. We were in the clear. In six months her weight was on track and she was a healthy and happy baby.

Jules and Michael have a very special relationship. She was the only child who had her father around the entire span of her life. Though our four kids are extremely close and loving toward one another (save for a few, but very typical stupid sibling fights), I think there is a natural resentment as a result of the bond Jules and her dad share. Michael is very involved in Julia's life. He does things with her, takes her places, and drives her everywhere. Because of our family's unique circumstances, the other three kids didn't get to experience that kind of fatherly closeness and involvement. I know it makes for some twinges of jealousy.

On the other hand, Jules always complains that she never experienced the tight-knit circle the other three kids shared when Michael was away and it was just us four at home. Sometimes I feel like our house is divided between Team Camille (Miq, Amanda, Michael Jr., and me) and Team Michael (Jules and Michael). Still, the older siblings are protective of our baby girl. She'll always be our baby.

 Sometimes repercussions don't always materialize immediately. That's what we've discovered in the last few years, particularly with the breakdown in the relationship between Michael Sr. and Michael Jr. It's been a long, hard road, not just between the two of them, but with the damage their conflict has inflicted on the entire family.

The enemy attacked us in this area to a breaking point, and I didn't know if our marriage was even going to survive. It seemed that the more successful and far-reaching Michael's ministry was, the more the devil dug his heels in, trying to destroy our family. While the relationship between my son and my husband has improved over the last few months (at the time of this writing), there was a long time when they were at each other's throats.

When Michael Jr. was accepted into the University of South Florida on a baseball scholarship, we were so proud of our boy. Because he was a late recruit, there was no available dorm space, so we paid for and furnished an apartment close to school.

A short time later, our son's coach called us out of the blue and told us "from one parent to another" that he thought it would be best if Michael came home. He wasn't meeting the expectations that were required of him to play ball. "I'm concerned," he told us. "On the field, Michael is amazing. Off the field, it's a different story." Continuing, the coach said that Michael had signed a contract at the beginning of the season promising to keep a B average in order to stay on the team. From our conversation, I sensed that my son was involved in something other than the average experimentation most college kids get involved with when they're away from home for the first time.

Before Michael came home from school, we noticed erratic behavior. One time we didn't hear from him for a few days, and then he called at three in the morning. He cried, mumbled, and slurred his words, barely managing to get out, "Come and get me, please, Mom," before hanging up and disappearing for a few more days. When we finally connected with him, Michael responded casually to our concern. "Sorry, Mom. I've been busy." We immediately booked him a flight home.

Back in California, my son wasn't the same young man who'd left for college a few months earlier. Something was off. Normally, he was the life of the party, always with a smile on his face and lots of energy in his step. But not anymore. At home, he was dark and sullen. He never wanted to be home and was always going out with his friends. When he was home, he hid in his room and sulked. His rebellious behavior got worse. He was smoking pot, drinking in excess, and even got a DUI.

Michael Jr. was hanging with his buddies one night, watching a basketball game and having a few beers. He was going to spend the night with one of his friends, but we were moving the next day, and he thought it would be best to come home. Well, a few beers were a few beers too many. Michael Jr. was on his cell phone and crashed into a guardrail. Aside from damaging his car, nothing and no one else was damaged or injured. A police car sat at the side of the road and witnessed the accident. My son was thrown in jail overnight and was released the next day on his own recognizance. It was a lesson my son (and his friends) will never forget. None of them even think of getting behind the wheel even after a couple of beers.

My husband was at his wit's end. He'd had enough of his son's irresponsible and destructive behavior. We sent him to stay with my brother Joaquin for about two months. Aside from Michael Jr.'s anger at us and his hurtful accusations that we were "throwing away the problem," in the long run, I know in my heart that the break helped. It helped my son detox from his harmful behaviors and get a fresh perspective on what he was doing with his life. But the trouble was far from over.

For two years after Michael Jr. returned from college, our house was infected with anger and bitterness. Darkness had kidnapped all signs of light, and as much as I tried, I couldn't find even the slightest glimmer of hope in our familial relationship. Those years were probably the hardest on our marriage because I felt I was being pulled like a rag doll between feuding father and son.

The two argued constantly. Michael Jr. got so enraged during these battles that he dared his father to take it a step further. "C'mon, Dad. Hit me. I dare you!" As a mother, being a witness to this kind of anger was heartbreaking.

The bulk of my son's anger stemmed from his dad's absence. When Michael Jr. was a little boy and his dad was home, they were the best of friends and spent a lot of time together. His dad coached him in baseball and basketball for many years. It hadn't always been turbulent. Michael Jr. had a lot of resentment pent up about his father because he was never around. He constantly complained, "You travel all over the country, speaking to so many different people, but you can't even talk to your own son." I don't think he was just referring to Michael's skyrocketing ministry and the fact that it did encompass a lot of time away from home. I felt that the consequences of a son having his father away in prison for many years had finally started to rear its ugly head. It was a hard truth to face.

My husband had a limited supply of patience when it came to his son. Michael Jr. was past the age of being scolded simply because he played with his food at the dinner table or put his feet on the coffee table. He was a young man emerging out of his late teens and dabbling in habits that could have long-term consequences. Michael didn't get his son's rebellion. He didn't get the lack of respect. He didn't get why he wasn't doing something positive with his life.

"Just get it together!" my husband would yell. "Start living your life like a man!" With as much passion, Michael Jr. would yell back, "Stop treating me like a jerk! You help all those other kids you preach to. Why is it so hard for you to show me the same kind of patience?"

I prayed so hard for God to work in both of their lives, though honestly I couldn't see how the relationship could be repaired. To me, it looked damaged beyond even the hand of Providence. The hearts of both father and son were shattered in a million tiny pieces. Could God really sweep into their lives and clean up the mess they had made? I wasn't so sure.

I left the carnage in God's hands and prayed, "Lord, I surrender this situation to You. I leave it in Your hands. Spirit, work in my husband and in my son's life and do what You need to do to bring some peace into our lives. I can't handle it anymore. I can't take it. Please, Lord, take this burden from me and intervene."

Not too long after, Michael Sr. came home one night from a speaking engagement and crawled into bed with me. I could tell something was bothering him, and I asked what was wrong. He began to share his heart with me.

"Right before I was getting on the stage to speak, I stood in the bathroom and was combing my hair. Suddenly, I stopped and started staring at myself in the mirror. I heard God speak in my spirit. He asked me, 'Have your ways been pleasing to the Lord with your son, Michael?' Cammy, my heart broke. I fell apart. I knew the answer to the question, and it wasn't a good one. It wasn't the answer that I knew would please God. I begged for forgiveness in that moment. Oh, Cammy, what have I done?"

My husband and I held each other for a long time that night and spent hours in prayer. It was the turning point in our family that would finally allow light, truth, and love to shine through the cracks and fissures of our relationship. God was chiseling through the iron bars that for too long had separated my husband from his son. He was beginning to do a work in their lives and in our family that He would ultimately be faithful to finish.

Though he and Michael Jr. still aren't chummy all the time, their relationship is certainly seeing more good days and fewer wrestling matches. My husband has learned to treat his son better. He gives more grace, love, patience, and room for our boy to grow. He refuses to allow Michael Jr. to provoke him into being angry or impatient. It's a change that was long overdue, and I'm grateful the devil was defeated in his evil scheme.

My son has made tremendous strides and continues to do so with a lot of love and prayer from us. He finished two years at Pierce College, where he played baseball and maintained a good grade point average. He had a role in a national commercial for Canon camera and made great money and is now working with his father selling merchandise. Michael Jr. hopes to attend culinary school soon.

I don't know what tomorrow holds for both of them, but I know this: God answers prayer. And I have faith that one day, what has been torn apart between father and son can be fully restored in a beautiful, mysterious, and grace-filled way that I cannot even imagine.

Amanda and Michael have always had a good relationship. When she was younger, she was Daddy's little helper. Maybe their connection has something to do with the fact that they are both alike. Both are a bit short-tempered, aggressive, and hardworking.

When Amanda was in high school, they temporarily clashed. This happened only when Michael didn't give her a specific reason for things he wanted her to do or not do (or she felt his reasons were not justified). Amanda would always ask, "Why?" and dive into a lengthy monologue about why she felt his demands were unfair.

She was persistent, and Michael balked at her need to share her opinion and express her feelings. This irritated Amanda even more. But when she finally learned that the best way to keep their relationship copasetic was for her to simply reply to his demands with a sweet "Yes, Dad," their disagreements stopped.

Her compliant attitude didn't mean she resigned her strong character. She continues to speak her mind—a little more softly to her dad, of course—and prides herself on being a risk taker. She's not afraid to take chances in life and has been very successful because of it.

Miq and Michael also shared a good relationship. Unlike Amanda, Miq is easygoing and avoids confrontation like the plague. Whenever she got in trouble as a little girl, she was always quick to say, "I'm sorry, Daddy" with her big, brown puppy-dog eyes. Michael would immediately forget why he was mad at her.

My oldest daughter had some rough times as a freshman in high school. She was beautiful, sweet, and popular, and a particular group of girls at school would torture her because of it. They picked on her and called her names, but she ignored them, refusing to counter their attacks with words or anything else.

I picked her up from school one day and remember how striking she looked walking toward the car in her cute cheerleading outfit. As she smiled and waved in my direction, out of nowhere a basketball was thrown at her. She barely missed getting smacked in the face. I immediately got out of the car to investigate where the ball had come from and noticed a group of girls laughing at their silly deed.

As a protective mama bear, I was dying to give them a piece of my mind, but Miq begged me to leave the girls alone (sound familiar?). On the ride home, she finally confided in me how she had been bullied for a while. It broke my heart, and I was ready to pull her out of school. Amanda knew about the trouble and was ready to go to bat for her in a heartbeat. Miq refused my suggestion and Amanda's protection. Eventually, as most things go, things smoothed out without Miq ever needing to defend herself.

I like to call Julia my "Elmer's Glue." During these two devastating years, she was the glue that held our family together. When the enemy was sleeping on our couch, deceiving us, and trying to convince us that our family was nothing but a hypocritical mess, our youngest daughter brought hope to our home. When I would hide in my bedroom and cry, even sometimes admitting that I wasn't sure I could go through with my marriage if the fighting continued, Jules would sit beside me and remind me that all families go through bad times.

She would hold my hand and tell me, "We have to keep praying, Mom. For Daddy, for Michael, for all of us." She was always encouraging her father and her brother to stop fighting and start praying. At the end of particularly vicious battles, Julia would visit with her dad and pray with him and then shuffle over to her brother's room to pray with him. She was my constant reminder that divorce wasn't an option and that with prayer and continued faith, God could work miracles and our family could (and would) see this storm through.

I had Julia at a pivotal time in my life. She was a miracle baby on so many different levels. Not only did she help me get through the family madness; she also helped me deal with the greatest loss in my life—my mother. Two years after Julia was born, my mother was diagnosed with breast cancer. And the battle began.

Miquelle's Christening (1985).
Mike went to prison shortly after.

My mom and sisters right before she died.
(L to R: Raquel, Me, Mom, Sabrina)

Me and the kids in 1992, while Mike
was in Lompac Federal Prison.

My precious Julia. She helped me cope
with the greatest loss in my life.

11

Choices and
God's Goodness

It was almost Valentine's Day in 2000. I sat in my car in the back parking lot of my kids' school, watching them run around the schoolyard as they anxiously waited for the final bell to ring. I was on edge. I knew my mom was going back to the doctor that day to get the results of her biopsy.

Only a few days earlier, she had called and told me she had found a big lump on her breast. Though she didn't act worried, I certainly was. And today she would find out what exactly the lump was. I don't know if it was my nerves or foreshadowing, but I couldn't shake the gnawing feeling of dread lurking in the pit of my stomach.

My cell phone rang just as the bell went off and the playground became a circus of screaming kids hightailing it out of the yard. "Hi, Cammy." My father was on the other line. He paused, then said, "Your mom has cancer."

Mom. Breast cancer. My heart took a nosedive, and I started to feel sick. I wanted to jump out of the car and scream, "Noooo!!" at the top of my lungs, but I noticed my kids were nearby, talking with their friends. I knew I had to compose myself.

My mom got on the phone, and I didn't even give her an opportunity to say anything. I jumped right in. "Mom, tell me everything. Don't keep anything from me."

She sounded tired. "Cam, it's true. I have breast cancer."

I swallowed the lump in my throat and reassured her that I would find her the best care at UCLA or Cedars-Sinai. She wasn't offering any more information, so I pestered her with questions. "Did the doctor say anything else? What do you have to do next?"

Mom sounded exasperated. "Cam, please stop. I don't know anything else. I'm telling you all I know. I have to go in for surgery soon. That's all I know. Cammy, we'll take this one day at a time. Okay? Everything is going to be all right."

I sat in shock listening to the obnoxious dial tone blare in my ear. My mom could have told me the same thing twenty times, but I still wouldn't have fully believed it. It couldn't be. It was impossible. My mom was in great health. Maybe the doctor was wrong. Maybe he didn't know what he was doing. Maybe he got the results mixed up with another patient's.

I was snapped back to reality by Amanda and Michael Jr. pounding on the car window. "Hell*ooo*!" they sarcastically whined. "Earth to Mother. Will you please open the door sometime this century?"

I groaned, "Get a grip, will you?" Kids could be so anxious. They hopped in the car, their voices hyper and loud, and noticed the stunned look on my face. As if on cue, they quieted down, respecting the fact that something pretty serious was probably on my mind.

I called Michael as soon as I got home, and right when he started to say, "Hi," I blurted out, "My mom has breast cancer."

"Oh, Cammy," he sighed. I could tell he was shaken up. "Everything is going to be okay, babe. We're going to find her the

best care and beat this thing." That night Michael and I began for-
mulating a game plan. We wanted my mom to have the best health
care possible. UCLA was our first choice, and Michael started making some phone calls.

The problem was, my mother didn't have any health insurance.

I was angry with myself. Over the years, I had given my mom
clothes, furniture, sent her on trips and to spas, and even helped
out with some of her household bills. Never once did it cross my
mind to get her health insurance. What was I thinking? Or, really,
why did I *not* think? I was flooded with regret. For hours, all I could
think about was what I could have or should have done.

While I was busy beating myself up, Michael saved the day. I
don't know how he did it, but he managed to procure my mother
health insurance, even though she had preexisting cancer. No
insurance company in their right mind would ever provide cov-
erage to someone with a serious disease, but Michael worked his
magic. The next few weeks were a blur of driving my mom to and
from the hospital, getting her ready to have the lump removed.

The day of surgery, my mom was surprisingly calm. I, on the
other hand, was a total wreck, but I put on an optimistic front, as
hard as it was at times.

As we moved closer to the big doors of the operating room, I
found myself unable to say anything except "I love you." The drugs
were settling in, and my mom's eyes started to flutter with sleep.
She nodded and smiled. "Pray, Cammy. Just pray. Everything is
going to be fine. I love you too." I was struck by how, though she
was the one in need and wavering between life and death, she was
trying to comfort me. How ironic.

My siblings, Michael, and my father crowded the waiting room
and nervously awaited my mother's arrival in the recovery room.
When she was wheeled in hours later, Michael and I were the first
ones by her side. Covered with IVs and connected to bleeping

machines that monitored her vital signs, my mom looked groggy. She tried to talk to us, but she didn't make much sense. "Rest up," I told her as I caressed her soft skin.

Dr. Helena Chang, my mom's surgeon, was a sharp woman who had a remarkable balance of toughness and compassion. She was the first to call us on the telephone in the recovery room. "Everything went even better than we expected," she began. "While the lump we found was at a stage 4, we were able to remove it without any complications. And after a thorough examination, we are happy to report that the cancer did not spread, even though that's generally the case for such a progressive stage. We also removed twelve lymph nodes, but they were all clear. Another great sign."

Dr. Chang paused to allow us a few seconds to soak in the information, then continued: "Cammy, your mom is going to be okay. There are a lot of positive things happening in her corner." I was so relieved I started thanking God right there in the middle of the cold recovery room, with a background of hospital beds, groaning postoperative patients, and nurses hustling about.

My father and I took her to her first chemo appointment. He couldn't bear to step into the room, so he stayed behind in the waiting room. From that day forward, he never went back; either Michael or I or both of us accompanied my mother for the rest of her appointments. Dad's absence wasn't an indication that he didn't love, care for, or support his wife. It was simply too much for him to bear. He couldn't handle the fact that his Irma was suffering from a disease that could very well take her life.

Mom was quiet as we waited for the chemo to work its magic. Before the procedure started, she asked me to pray that it would be the blood of Jesus flowing through her veins instead of the poison. My mom went in for treatment every other day for about two weeks. She had a number of tests, and after a while, she seemed to be doing very well. For about a year, my mother was safe in the arms of remission.

The following April, my sister Sabrina called me. She sounded frantic. "Cammy, I was driving Mom back to her house when she had a seizure in the car. One minute we were talking, and the next minute she lost it. She was like a zombie. I don't know how it happened. She just blacked out and didn't remember a thing." My heart sank. I didn't want to expect the worst, but the same sinking feeling I'd had when I first found out the results of my mom's biopsy made an encore appearance.

Sabrina continued her verbal frenzy, talking a hundred miles a minute. "So I took her to the emergency room at Anaheim Memorial. They gave her a brain scan." I heard her swallow back tears. "Cammy, the doctor told her something was going on in her brain, and whatever it was didn't just show up; it has been there for a while."

Sabrina was advised to take our mom and the brain scans to her doctor as quickly as possible. When my sister looked at the X-rays, she told me about the many white spots that dotted Mom's brain. We both suspected it was cancer, but no one wanted to voice that feeling.

Michael called me a short time later. He had been in New York. I told him what happened and that we were pretty sure the cancer had spread to her brain. He refused to jump to any conclusions and told me, "Let's just wait until we see the doctor tomorrow." Premature assumption or not, I knew it was cancer. Strangely enough, Michael had also received some bad news about a parent only a few hours earlier. His father had been arrested earlier in the day for violating his parole. Needless to say, this was not a good day for the Franzese family.

We were right about our assumptions. When we found out the diagnosis, I felt like someone had thrown a dagger into my chest at top speed. I didn't want to imagine what would happen if there was nothing medical science could do to kill the cancer indefinitely. I didn't want to imagine the pain and suffering my mom would have to endure while the disease slowly spread throughout every organ in her body. But more so, I didn't want to imagine living the rest of my life without my mom.

Days after we learned that cancer was attacking my mom's brain, I turned to Michael for comfort. "My mom's going to die, isn't she?"

Michael shook his head. "No, she's not, Cammy. Absolutely not."

I knew his heart was in the right place, but I also knew it was a superficial answer, an empty promise spoken just to make me feel better in the moment. Michael was a fighter by nature. It was who he was. But I believe he knew inwardly that this was one fight we would not win.

I remember sitting with my mom and Michael in the radiologist's office for an update on her condition. At that point, she had finished undergoing a few radiation treatments. She wore a helmet during these procedures, which served to localize the radiation to the area of her brain that was affected by the cancer.

After shuffling some papers around her desk, the radiologist looked up and cleared her throat. "I'm sorry. There's nothing further we can do. It's just a matter of time." She turned toward my mother. "Irma, do you want to know how much time you have left?"

What a horrible question. What a horrible conversation, for that matter. I couldn't believe I was sitting in some fancy office, listening to a woman in a starchy, white coat offer my mom her prediction of when she would die.

Mom shook her head and looked the doctor straight in the eye. In a quiet but firm voice, she told her, "No. I don't want to know, because the truth is, Doctor, you really don't even know. Only God knows when my time is up."

The doctor nodded and looked at us with a deep sadness. "You're right," she told my mother. "Take things one day at a time."

Before the three of us left her office, she wished us luck. As if luck had anything to do with this.

Though the report was grim, my mom was ecstatic at not having to deal with any more radiation. She threw the helmet in the car and climbed into the front seat. "I am so glad I'm done with that silly thing." A smile broke out on her face.

"You're bringing it home?" I asked.

"It's my parting gift. You can keep it, Cammy. Put it in your memory box," she said, laughing. (I actually did keep the helmet for a long time after she passed away. But when it became too much of a painful reminder, I threw it in the trash.)

Even though that meeting hadn't ended on a happy note, I wasn't discouraged by the doctor's bad report. None of us were. We all held on to hope, to possibility, to maybes. I believed God was going to intervene and give my mother the miracle she deserved. I knew she wouldn't live forever, but I didn't think it was her time to go just yet. There was still so much to do, so much to say. My mom felt the same way. She was still confident that God was going to save her.

Mom began having frequent hallucinations. One time she started saying, "Jesus, where are You? Are You there?" My sister was by her side at the time and ran out to come find me. She was shaking. "I think Mom's dying," she kept repeating over and over like a broken record. A few days later, though she had lived with Michael and me for a while, we took our mother back home to Anaheim, knowing she was in the final stages of her life. She loved her little house. There was nothing she enjoyed more than being in her safe haven. And it didn't look like a miracle was on its way, anyway.

Michael and I and the rest of the siblings took turns taking care of my mother along with a rotating shift of hospice nurses.

The men and women who worked with my mom were amazing. I found them to be some of the most compassionate people I've ever encountered in my life.

From the afternoon my mom was diagnosed with breast cancer to the morning she took her last breath, she never complained. She never cried. She never blamed God. She never got sad. She never questioned why she had to suffer. My mother was surrounded by an inexplicable peace, indicative, of course, of her tremendous faith. She didn't allow the negative of a deadly disease to intrude on her oasis of God-given serenity.

Whenever I mentioned I was worried about her, especially if she was having a bad day and was in a lot of pain, she was quick to hush me up. She didn't want me to worry about her or about the possibility of her dying. Her words were always full of comfort and compassion, and she never hesitated to point out her confidence in God, that even in the face of this terrible illness, He was present. Faithful. And He would help us all through the heartbreaking journey.

When she was at UCLA, we spoke twice about her passing. Our last conversation was when she was only days away from leaving this earth. She said, "Cammy, don't worry about me. I'm not afraid of dying. I know it's sad because it's so final, but it's only the beginning of seeing the beauty of God."

I held her hand tight as she continued. Tears brimmed her eyes. "I don't want to die; I'll miss you and all my children and grandkids more than I can say. I'm heartbroken over the pain I know you will all go through. It kills me that I can't spare you from that grief. But I also know that if it is God's will for me to die, He will be there for all of you and see you through."

I nodded, choking back my tears. It broke my heart to witness the power of the disease and see my mother so helpless, confined to a bed and covered with a spidery web of IVs. She clutched a morphine drip in her right hand, her only immediate relief from the crushing pain. I sat on the edge of the bed and inched as close to my mom's emaciated body as I could without crushing her. I caressed her gaunt face and rubbed her temples.

All I could do was whisper how much she meant to me, even though the string of vowels and consonants couldn't adequately communicate the love and appreciation I had in my heart for her. "I love you, Mom. You are the best mother that anyone could ask for. Thank you for being a wonderful mom, wife, and woman. You are such a blessing to me. Mom, I want you to know that it's an honor to be your daughter and to take care of you in your time of need. Thank you for giving me that privilege."

A tiny tear slipped down her wrinkled cheek. She reached out and gave my hand a slight squeeze, as much as she could muster, and mouthed, "I love you, Cammy." It was a beautiful moment, one I will never forget. But it was also the moment I knew was the beginning of the end.

Mom died a week later. The last two days before my mother passed away, her breathing was unusually shallow and her feet were as cold as ice, even with my frequent massages and the wool socks Michael had bought for her. The morning she died, she was barely conscious.

She was never alone. All her kids and their spouses sat by her side, praying and crying. We knew she would pass at any moment. Her feet were getting colder by the minute. We held hands and sang her favorite songs, like "Amazing God," "Lead Me to the Cross," and her favorite, "Healing Oil." It was our peace offering to her, our way of giving her permission to leave this world. With tears in our eyes, one by one, my brothers and sisters held my mother's hand and whispered their final good-byes in her ear.

I briefly left the room when I was startled by the sound of a voice yelling, "Hurry! Get back inside! I think Mom's taking her last breath." I ran and joined the circle that had formed around her bed of those who loved her without fail. Sabrina knelt down beside my mother and whispered in her ear, "It's okay for you to go, Mom. We love you so much, and we'll all see you again." With her last bit of strength, our mother clasped her hand over her heart and her last tear cascaded down her face.

We watched her chest heave up, then fall back silent into her body. That was it. She had gone home. The hospice nurse looked at his watch and quietly announced the time of death. He later told us he had never before witnessed such a beautiful parting of a loved one.

An eerie but not uncomfortable silence enveloped the room for a minute. And then the floodgates opened. We cried. We sobbed. We held each other. Some of my siblings knelt beside my mother and laid their heads on her bed, in disbelief; others did it for comfort, to be as close to her as possible for the last time.

In a matter of seconds, the reality hit me like a hammer on an anvil. I quietly left the room and ran out the front door of my parents' house. Grief poured over me in a tsunami of tears. I never sobbed so hard in my life. Not even when Michael went back to prison for another four years. Not even when I miscarried what would have been my fourth child. Not even when I found out my mother had cancer.

Michael was outside, and I collapsed in his arms. He later told me he was afraid I was going to faint, I was so distraught. It was comforting to be held by my husband, but even that couldn't soothe the wounds of losing a mother. After a few minutes, he was able to calm me down, and we went back into the house. I was so upset I could barely walk and held on to him for dear life.

My brother Joaquin asked Michael to leave the room so the "Skeleton Crew" could have one final moment with their mom. I know my husband was a little taken aback by the request, but while I felt bad, I understand where Joaquin was coming from. Yes, my husband did deserve to be in the room, but Joaquin was a young kid who had just lost his mother and best friend, and he didn't ask Michael to leave to intentionally hurt his feelings. He only wanted to have some time reserved just for my mom and her babies.

I am forever grateful to Michael for his unflagging effort and the love he gave my mother during our whole marriage, but especially when she was sick. He went far and above what I could ever ask for. I love him so much for that. And I know my mother appreciated his acts of love and kindness as much as I did. My husband is a special man, and during one of the hardest times of my life, he was there for my mom and me in so many amazing ways that spoke volumes about his character.

When the ambulance arrived to take my mother's body, Michael carried her frail, ninety-pound frame in his arms as the red lights from the vehicle lit up the yard like a Christmas tree. My siblings and I watched the ambulance pull away, and we wailed for hours, still in shock that our precious mother had left this world.

My mother's death rocked my faith more than any troublesome or tragic event that happened in my life. She was a godly, kind, compassionate, and selfless woman who suffered extensively. The pain, the medications that made her sick, the intolerable aches, the exhaustion, the constant vomiting—all these ailments hammered away at her physical body, taking with it jagged pieces of strength, yet she never uttered a complaint. "Jesus suffered," she said. "Who are we not to suffer? Why should I feel sorry for myself when He went through more than I did?" Even in her last days, my mom touted her strong faith, not by her words, but by her actions—the truest example, I believe, of what a believer should be.

When loved ones pass away, many of us are left with guilt. We may feel guilty about the decisions we've had to make for them or how their journey trying to recover or heal elapsed. It's easy to be shadowed by what-if questions, but it doesn't benefit us at all. And it certainly won't bring them back.

Fighting for our dying loved ones comes from a place of genuine love. We innately want to fight for their survival—we want them to beat the odds—and chances are, we do whatever we can, even taking extreme measures so they can hold on and live as long as possible. I know. It's what I did for my mom. But years later, the guilt of what I did and didn't do just about tore me up.

I was plagued with questions like, "Why didn't I let her eat whatever she wanted?" "Why did I make her take those horse-pill vitamins?" "Why didn't I tell her to take more relaxing baths?" "Why didn't I make her fight harder?" Why? Why? *Why?*

I was in church one morning when the Lord spoke to my heart through a simple line in a beautiful worship song, "Your love, Lord, is better than life." Right then I remembered that my mother was in a better place, a kingdom far beyond ours. A kingdom without tears, pain, suffering, doubt, and emptiness. A kingdom of peace, rest, comfort, health, fullness, and joy unspeakable.

I felt God telling me that in every situation, even my mother's passing, He is in control, and He knows best. I tried so hard to save my mother, and though God allowed me to take whatever desperate measure I could to get her better, He knew what He was doing and that He had already saved her. In my mother's life and in her death, she knew that truth. She knew God was in the driver's seat and ultimately His hands, not mine, would guide her journey.

Before she passed away, my mom reminded me not to blame my father for her life. In her last days she could sense my growing frustration with him. Dad's past behaviors particularly stung because my mom was the one suffering; it seemed so unfair for someone as faithful and steadfast as she was. Yet as her life slowly ebbed away, she kept prompting me to forgive, to let go, to move on. But my stubborn attitude wouldn't budge; I didn't want to be so quick to forget the past. Mom was persistent. "Don't blame your father for my life. Marrying and staying with him was the choice that I made. Just love him and pray him into heaven."

My father was very private in his mourning. He wore dark sunglasses for three weeks straight so no one would notice his bloodshot eyes. I believe he was burdened by guilt for a long time. Recently he started sharing stories with me about how very much in love he was with my mother. It was almost like he was trying to convince me that their relationship wasn't all bad. Though, growing up, I don't remember seeing a lot of intimate moments between them, maybe I just didn't notice.

I'll never forget the vivid memory I have of the two of them together before my mother died. I walked into my parents' house one afternoon and saw my mom eating a burrito. It was so big my dad had to help her hold it in place so the wrap wouldn't fall apart in her lap. I watched them for a few seconds before they noticed I was there. My mom looked surprised, like a schoolgirl who got caught stealing a kiss from her boyfriend. Here she was, eating a pile of grease, basically a heart attack wrapped in a tortilla, when I had her on a strict, macrobiotic diet. But I didn't care about what I thought was a nutritionally poor choice of lunch. I was touched by the intimacy of my dad helping my mom eat her burrito. I saw love in action between them that day, and that tender moment will forever be ingrained in my memory.

My father is a different man today than he was when I was growing up. Recently, in an act of great humility, he even apologized for not being the best husband or father and told me he wished he had been a better man. He is still active with the César Chávez organization but devotes more of himself and his time to his grandchildren. I like to say that whatever he lacked as a father, he makes up for as a grandfather. The kids love him.

My dad works tirelessly to make his grandkids' lives better. He coaches their basketball teams, attends their every sporting event, drives them wherever they need to go, and he even gives them his last dollar if they need it. I believe this is his way of showing my mom how grateful and blessed he was to be her husband.

I don't believe my father ever meant to hurt her or us, I think he raised us in a way that stood for revolution, fighting the system he hated. While all of us respected what he was trying to do, none of us agreed with the method of his madness. His heart was in the right place, but his actions weren't always in our best interests. But we knew he loved us, and we certainly loved him.

My mother's prayers for my father were eventually answered. After her passing, he came to know the Lord and now attends church every week. There is power in prayer. Even though what we pray for may not always come to pass in our time, God is forever faithful.

I love the saying, "If you want to make God laugh, tell Him your plans." It reminds me of Michael's decision to quit the Mob, the decision he said he made for me. It didn't take long for God to reshape the root of that decision in a life-changing way. Michael's plan was to spend his life with me, but God's plan was different. He knew Michael wasn't just surrendering his past for me; he would ultimately be living his life for God.

I'm not going to lie. The unique road I've traveled hasn't been easy. My marriage and my life is proof that you have to deal with and make the most out of not just the inevitable happenstances of life, but more important, the consequences that stem from the choices we make. I like what Eleanor Roosevelt said: "In the long run, we shape our lives, and we shape ourselves. The process never ends until we die. And the choices we make are ultimately our own responsibility."

Just as my mother made her choices in life and accepted responsibility for them, so did I. I made the choice to marry an ex-mobster. I chose to marry Michael even when he was on trial for tax evasion and racketeering and even when I had an inkling that his past was more colorful than I wanted to imagine. But that didn't mean God wasn't beyond putting His divine fingerprints on our lives. Because that's what happened. God worked in us and through us so our lives could be a witness to His forgiveness, His mercy, His goodness, and His love. It's like the apostle Paul said, "And we know that God causes everything to work together for the good of those who love God and are called according to his purpose for them" (Romans 8:28).

You may be in a situation where life hasn't turned out as magically as you had hoped. Maybe it's for reasons that were out of your control, or maybe because you made some poor choices. Be encouraged. God can work through your situation to bring about amazing things, things that you can't even dream up on your own. Things that only God, in His infinite power, can do.

Trust Him. Give Him your heart. Give Him your everything. Take His hand and let Him lead you through your shadows and valleys. Peace will come. Restoration will come. But only if you trust God and surrender your heart and your life to Him.

Maybe you're in a marriage and are contemplating divorce, for whatever reason. God didn't promise us the perfect relationships that are portrayed on TV shows where conflicts are resolved in twenty-two minutes. Newness, romance, and the butterflies you feel when you first fall in love will fade. The fluffy side of love rises and falls, like the peaks and valleys of a mountain.

I want to encourage you to not only work on your relationship with your spouse (it should be something you do every day), but to also work on your relationship with God. Pray. Pray without ceasing. And don't just deepen your walk with the Lord by talking to Him. Listen. Sometimes we just have to be quiet and still. I've found that when we are attuned to God's Spirit, He really does speak and reveal truth to us.

This is especially important if you are not married but are dating someone or contemplating getting married. Be sure the man you are in a relationship with is the man God wants for you. Pray that you pledge your heart to the man that God has chosen for you.

Above all else, seek God first. Don't make the mistake of putting others, even a great husband, above God. "Seek the Kingdom of God above all else, and live righteously, and he will give you everything you need" (Matthew 6:33). My mother took this verse to heart, and I encourage my daughters to do the same. I don't care how much money is in your bank account, what kind of car you drive, how pretty you are, or what an incredible husband you are blessed to have; if you don't have a relationship with God, it doesn't matter.

When you are stripped of all of your material securities, you quickly learn where your dependence lies. I know I did. And I thank God I was given a chance to realign my allegiance with Him and make Him the Lord over my life. Because really, that's what life is about, being connected with Him. I know that with God by my side, I really can do all things, go through all things, and endure all things.

And dear friend, I promise you—so can you.

Shooters in Fort Lauderdale, where Mike
and I had our first date.

My beautiful family, Christmas (2010).

April 5, 2000

No weapon can form againts us, no weapon can form againts us!! This I repeat because I know its true! Nothing that is evil can proper againts us, if God is with us who can be againts us? no one Nothing can seperate us from the Love of Jesus Christ. Lord thank you for all you've done in my life I know this cancer is your battle, not mine, I surrender it to you thank you for giving me a family and friends who Love me unconditionally, even when I fail them, you never do! I want to thank Dr. Gordon for his kindness + true compassion he was and is a good man

. . . more than this day.

to Michael my Son in Law
for his concern and never
ending research on my cancer and for helping me to
get the help I needed, he went
beyond what he had to do, and
I am greatful, I hope to be
back at work soon at California tires, I enjoy talking to
Chrissy and I like to be useful.
I am thankful for all your tears
and concern, I'm sorry I put
you through, so much, I hope
you know how much I Love
you and how I hope you would
slow down on your life, and
stop everyday onetofive moretimes
daily to know that God is God
take time to listen to him
daily, He is energy to your
soul

Nothing is worth . . .

My brother Rudy and Lupe
& Children Moses & Adelita
came to visit it was very
pleasant, they brought me
a lovely floral piece that, its
on my beautiful long dresser Sabrina
got for me, its gorgeous and
everyone that sees it compliments
it, thank's Sabrina, you know
what I like!! Lord thank
you for sending Janice over
with fresh washed fruit
it was so nice of her, even
though she's ready to have that
child, she thought about me.
Thank you for all the prayers
and good thoughts

. . . more than this day.

Epilogue

For the better part of my life, I would never have dreamed of revealing my life story as I have in the pages of this book. For several years I resisted my husband's encouragement to join in his ministry and to "tell my story to the world." I have always considered my innermost thoughts about my faith, my marriage, and my family to be very private. I believed that God's purpose for my life was to devote myself to caring for my husband and raising our four children. Although I fervently supported my husband's ministry, I felt that I should do so quietly, from the confines of our home. I would serve not only as Michael's companion, but also as his accountability partner. At times, that proved to be a very challenging task.

There is no doubt my husband loves the Lord and that his desire is to serve God fervently. Over the years I have seen him evolve into a dynamic evangelist and faithful servant of Jesus Christ. There were times, however, that the enemy used the influence of Michael's past life against him. When I would see him revert to his old ways of dealing with certain issues, I would firmly let him know his actions were unacceptable both to God and to me and, believe it or not, he would listen. At least most of the time.

Michael has often made the statement, "You can take the boy out of Brooklyn, but you can't always take Brooklyn out of the boy." I find that to be a very revealing statement. Radical changes in a person's life do not come easy. They are part of the process of coming to God through a relationship with Jesus Christ. I do believe that God placed me in Michael's life, not only to bring him to the Lord, but also to keep him in the Lord as he matured in his faith and developed the ministry the Holy Spirit ordained for him. I feel he is now firmly a servant of God and I have fulfilled my purpose in helping to bring him along. Of course, I will continue to serve God in that regard.

Throughout the years, after sharing his testimony at a church service or ministry event, Michael often told me people out there needed to hear from me. He would tell me that his ministry is really "our ministry" and he believed there was a calling on my life as well as on his to encourage people to seek the Lord's guidance in their relationships and in their marriages. As his ministry continued to grow, Michael felt God's calling on my life growing stronger and he continued to encourage me to pray about making a more public profession of my faith.

Several months ago I accompanied Michael to a ministry event in Honolulu, Hawaii. Within moments after the service ended I was surrounded at the product table by a group of some twenty young women very eager to talk with me. Apparently, they were all either in a relationship with a so-called "bad boy," or were attracted to one. After hearing Michael talk about me during his testimony, they believed I was in a marriage with the "ultimate bad boy" and wanted my advice on how to have a godly relationship with theirs.

I ministered to these young women for almost an hour, answering their questions and encouraging them to seek God first in their relationships. I was overwhelmed by my apparent impact on them. God used these young women to further encourage me to share what the Lord has done in my life and in my marriage. I have had similar experiences with women of all ages at subsequent ministry events. Those encounters, along with Michael's continuous encouragement moved me to go forward with this writing. I hope this book will be another step toward the fulfillment of God's purpose for my life.

Our children were all surprised when I agreed to write the book. They were familiar with their father having a very public persona, but always knew me to be a very private person. I pray sharing my story will encourage our daughters to fulfill the plan and purpose God has for their lives.

At the time of this writing all my children are, thankfully, doing well. Miquelle is working with Michael in his ministry and plans to attend graduate school and pursue a career in the medical field. Michael and I are very proud of the young woman she has become. She has a wonderful spirit and I know that when God's calling becomes a burning in her heart, she will be a dynamic and faithful servant.

Amanda is currently on the island of Samoa working on the production of ABC's adventure reality series Survivor. After graduating from college she worked for the television production company that Michael works with, which led to her work on the successful series. Although she is doing extremely well in the entertainment field, she plans to return to graduate school and pursue her career in law. I have no doubt she will be successful. She is very much like her father, determined to succeed at whatever she sets her mind to. Although Michael encourages her to pursue a career in law, he jokes that he hopes to never require her legal services. I can certainly understand that.

Michael Jr. appears determined to put his past struggles behind him. He is currently working in a restaurant, preparing to attend culinary school and turn his passion for cooking into a career. He wants to one day open a restaurant of his own—Italian, of course. Best of all, his relationship with Michael has greatly improved. Father and son appear to have finally come to terms with one another. I am so grateful to the Lord for answering my prayers in that regard. Michael and I believe our son will one day join his father in the ministry and we continue to keep him in prayer.

Our daughter Julia has just become a teenager and continues to be such a joy in our lives. She is avidly pursuing her passion for dance. The many years Julia spent training and performing at Mn'R Dance Academy under the expert tutelage of choreographer and friend, Roni Blak, seem to have paid off. Julia recently auditioned for and was accepted into one of the most elite dance programs in the country at Mather School of Dance in Orange County, California. I am so very proud of her. A good part of my days are spent driving her to dance classes and auditions, supporting her and providing her with the tools she needs to succeed in such a career. I must admit there are times when I can be tough on Julia. She is so gifted, I am constantly pushing her to do her best. I forget she is only thirteen and sometimes just wants to act like a typical young teenage girl. Michael is quick to come to her defense and remind me how I would "correct" him when he would get on Michael Jr. when he slacked off in sports. Funny how we see things differently when the shoe lands on the other foot. I am doing my best to give Julia her space when she needs it and I do believe I am making progress. God's timing in blessing Michael and me with Julia was perfect. She has been my constant companion while Michael continues to travel extensively in furtherance of his ministry. I am so grateful to God for blessing me with all our children.

What lies ahead for our family in the years to come? A movie based on our life story as it is told in Michael's autobiography, Blood Covenant, is scheduled for production later this year. I have learned that nothing in the film business is a sure thing until the cameras actually roll, but it appears that this production is going forward. Although the story of Michael's life in the mob will be told, Michael has assured me and the thousands of people he ministers to each week that the movie will honor God and will serve to further the purpose of his ministry. I believe God will honor Michael's heart and, if the project succeeds in going forward, it will be a further testimony of what God can do. Like all else in our lives, I am keeping this project in prayer. It is ironic that Michael and I began our lives together on the set of a movie and now the story of our lives will be told in a movie. The Lord certainly does work in mysterious ways at times.

Although I will always support Michael in his ministry and share our story when it is appropriate to do so, I do not see myself in full-time ministry. That is my husband's calling. Besides, being married to Michael is in itself a full-time ministry. Rarely in the past twenty-six years has there been a dull moment and I am confident that will not change any time soon. I know the Lord wants me to continue to support my husband and to keep him accountable to what God wants him to do.

I have learned never to try to out-plan God. It is far better to pray for God's will to be done than to try to impose our wants and desires on Him. I will do my best to be obedient and to continue to fulfill the purpose He has for my life—whatever that might be and wherever it may lead. I am grateful He has given me the opportunity to share a part of my story with you. I am hopeful there will be more to share in the future.

Thank you and may God bless you!

Acknowledgments

There are so many people to thank for being a part of my life story and for making it worthy of sharing it. I would like to mention just a few.

A special thanks to my agent and friend, Esther Federokevich, for believing in me and encouraging me to move forward with the book.

Thank you to Amy Gregory Spence, my cowriter, for the countless hours we spent together in writing the book. I truly appreciate her hard work and her ability to get to the heart of the story. Without her effort and dedication, I could never have undertaken this project and seen it through to completion. Thank you so much, Amy.

I want to thank the staff at Thomas Nelson, especially Joel Miller, Kristen Parrish, and Heather Skelton, for believing in me and for all their help in making the book happen. Your collective efforts are most appreciated.

I want to thank my children for supporting my efforts and encouraging me to move forward. A special thanks to my daughter Julia, who spent countless hours waiting for me while Amy and I worked on the manuscript. She was there to keep me company every step of the way. Thank you, sweetheart. Mommy is so grateful to you for being there with me.

A very special thank you to my husband, Michael, who has been encouraging me for years to write this book. Your participation and help with the writing was invaluable throughout the process. I now have a greater appreciation for the effort you put forth in writing your own books. Thank you, honey.

I want to thank God for giving me a life story that others consider worthy to write about. You are truly an awesome God and I pray readers who don't know You will come to know You through the pages of this book. Thank you, God!